2 CORINTHIANS

THE CALL TO RECONCILIATION

DR. DAVID JEREMIAH

Prepared by Peachtree Publishing Services

THOMAS NELSON
Since 1798

2 Corinthians
Jeremiah Bible Study Series

© 2019 by Dr. David Jeremiah

Published in Nashville, Tennessee, by Thomas Nelson. Thomas Nelson is a registered trademark of HarperCollins Christian Publishing, Inc.

Produced with assistance of Peachtree Publishing Service (www.PeachtreePublishingServices.com). Project staff include Christopher D. Hudson, Randy Southern, and Peter Blankenship.

All Scripture quotations are taken from The Holy Bible, New King James Version. Copyright © 1979, 1980, 1982 by Thomas Nelson. All rights reserved.

Thomas Nelson titles may be purchased in bulk for educational, business, fundraising, or sales promotional use. For information, please e-mail SpecialMarkets@ThomasNelson.com.

ISBN 978-0-310-09748-8

Second Printing February 2021 / Printed in the United States of America

24 25 26 27 28 LBC 8 7 6 5 4

CONTENTS

Introduction to the Letter of 2 Corinthians v

LESSON 1 A Question of Sincerity (*2 Corinthians 1:1–24*) 1
LESSON 2 Identified with Christ (*2 Corinthians 2:1–3:18*) 13
LESSON 3 Treasure in Earthen Vessels (*2 Corinthians 4:1–18*) 25
LESSON 4 The Gospel of Reconciliation (*2 Corinthians 5:1–21*) 37
LESSON 5 Unequally Yoked (*2 Corinthians 6:1–18*) 49
LESSON 6 Speaking the Truth in Love (*2 Corinthians 7:1–16*) 61
LESSON 7 How to Give (*2 Corinthians 8:1–24*) 73
LESSON 8 Sowing and Reaping (*2 Corinthians 9:1–15*) 85
LESSON 9 The Spiritual War (*2 Corinthians 10:1–18*) 95
LESSON 10 God Is Our Strength (*2 Corinthians 11:1–33*)......... 105
LESSON 11 God's Grace in Our Weakness (*2 Corinthians 12:1–21*) .. 117
LESSON 12 Examine Yourselves (*2 Corinthians 13:1–14*)......... 127

Leader's Guide 137
About Dr. David Jeremiah and Turning Point 143
Stay Connected to Dr. David Jeremiah 145

INTRODUCTION TO
The Letter of 2 Corinthians

"O Corinthians! We have spoken openly to you, our heart is wide open. You are not restricted by us, but you are restricted by your own affections" (2 Corinthians 6:11–12). The apostle often found it necessary to "speak openly" to the believers in Corinth. The letters he wrote to the congregation (including the epistle we recognize as 1 Corinthians) often contained strongly worded arguments and difficult truths for the believers to accept. Inevitably, his words offended some of the factions in the church . . . who turned on Paul by questioning his authority as an apostle and his sincerity toward them. This put Paul in a delicate position. He had no reason to apologize, for he had done nothing wrong, but he was deeply concerned about the believers' wellbeing and salvation, so he did not want to alienate them. Paul's second letter to the believers in Corinth represents his masterful solution to the problem

AUTHOR AND DATE

The writer of this letter identifies himself as Paul (see 1:1 and 10:1), and the epistle contains a number of details about his life that fit with what we know of the apostle based on his other letters and the book of Acts. Although the letter appears to have been unknown to Clement of Rome, an early church father who lived c. AD 35–99, it was quoted by other early church leaders, including Polycarp (c. AD 105), Irenaeus (c. AD 185), and Tertullian (c. AD 210). Today, nearly every biblical scholar agrees with the early church's claim that the apostle penned the letter. It is likely that

Paul wrote the epistle shortly after 1 Corinthians, in the fall of AD 56, from somewhere in the region of Macedonia—most likely the city of Philippi.

BACKGROUND AND SETTING

Paul arrived in Corinth during his second missionary journey, c. AD 52, and ministered in the city for a year and a half. After departing, Paul wrote the letter of 1 Corinthians, c. AD 55, from the city of Ephesus and sent Titus, his fellow minister, to deliver it to the church. It appears the believers corrected many of the abuses Paul called out in that letter, but a new problem arose when a faction arrived from Palestine (known as the Judaizers) and began to again create divisions in the church. This prompted Paul to pay a "painful visit" to the believers in Corinth. After he left, he was again criticized by the anti-Pauline faction, which prompted him to write a "severe letter" to the church. Paul must have wondered how the believers would take this letter, but his fears were allayed when Titus arrived and said it had been well received. In gratitude, Paul penned 2 Corinthians 1–9 during further ministry work in Macedonia . . . and then learned the faction against him was still trying to undermine his authority. In response, Paul penned 2 Corinthians 10–13 and sent Titus to deliver both parts to the struggling church.

KEY THEMES

Several key themes are prominent in Paul's second letter to the Corinthians. The first is that *there is a cost in following Christ.* In Paul's absence, false teachers had journeyed to Corinth and were attacking his authority as an apostle. In response, Paul outlines the price he often paid in service to Christ and the gospel (see 1:8–11; 6:3–13; 11:22–29) and models forgiveness for one individual in particular who had spoken against him (see 2:3–11). Paul's listings of hardships reminds us of Jesus' warning about the cost of being a true disciple (see Luke 14:25–33).

A second theme is that *followers of Christ have been reconciled with God.* Paul provides a concise summary midway through the letter of what it means to be made right with God. When we choose to put our faith in Christ, we become a new creation in Him—the old nature passes away and we embrace the new life of righteousness that God has for us. Once we experience this new life, we are compelled to become "ambassadors for Christ" and share the message of reconciliation with the world (see 2 Corinthians 5:12–6:2).

A third theme is that *believers have a responsibility to give to others* (see 8:1–9:15). One of Paul's main causes was a collection that he was taking up among the Gentile churches for the believers in Jerusalem. These Jewish followers of Christ had been subjected to persecution, ostracized from society, and were suffering from a famine in the region. For Paul, it was the duty of those who had been given much from God to share those resources with others in need. His instructions to the believers in the matter provide us with the most detailed description of sacrificial and generous giving found anywhere in his epistles.

A fourth theme is in regard to t*he characteristics that should define a leader in the church*. Paul understood that the attacks against him were the result of Satan's attempts to undermine the work of the gospel. So he called on the believers to recognize that this was taking place and then outlined the traits that should define a person who claimed to represent Christ in leadership. For Paul, boldness in defending the gospel and boasting in the grace of Christ set apart true godly leaders from those who operate out of more carnal motives (see 10:1–12:10).

KEY APPLICATIONS

All too often, believers today have preconceived ideas of what the Christian life should look like. We picture a care-free existence . . . when the Bible promises just the opposite. In this letter, the apostle Paul helps us change this mindset by providing examples from his own life to reveal what it means to be a true follower of Christ—a road that includes pain, trials, obstacles, and suffering. But it is a road that in the end is worth all the struggle, for we have the promise from God that those who travel it faithfully will receive the gift of eternal life.

LESSON *one*

A QUESTION OF SINCERITY

2 Corinthians 1:1–24

GETTING STARTED

How can you tell if someone is being sincere in their actions toward you?

_____

_____

_____

_____

_____

_____

_____

_____

_____

_____

_____

_____

_____

_____

_____

_____

_____

_____

_____

SETTING THE STAGE

If you have ever been reprimanded for something you did, you have a good idea of how many of the believers in Corinth felt after their interactions with Paul. The apostle never minced words when he confronted the believers about their spiritual immaturity and their tolerance for idolatry and sexual immorality. Needless to say, many of the church members did not receive the admonitions in the spirit in which they were intended.

As a group, the Corinthians had a fairly high opinion of themselves—and a surprisingly low opinion of Paul. Complicating matters further was the fact that many in the church believed they had a legitimate claim against the apostle. Paul had wanted to visit them and had even promised to make the trip. However, certain complications had prevented this from happening.

The first of these was a life-threatening event in Asia. The apostle Paul offers few details about the specifics concerning this event, but it had a devastating effect on him—prompting him to despair "even of life" (1:8). The second complication was Paul's realization that his relationship with the Corinthians had deteriorated to the point that a personal visit would have been counterproductive. So he tells them plainly, "I call God as witness against my soul, that to spare you I came no more to Corinth" (1:23).

Factions in the Corinthian church had seized on the apostle Paul's decision not to follow through on his original plan. They had accused him of being insincere. Paul's rivals on the itinerant speaking circuit added fuel to the fire for their own gain. They thought they had Paul backed into a corner. What they failed to realize was that Paul had the truth—God's truth—on his side.

EXPLORING THE TEXT

Comfort in Suffering (2 Corinthians 1:1–7)

> [1] Paul, an apostle of Jesus Christ by the will of God, and Timothy our brother,

To the church of God which is at Corinth, with all the saints who are in all Achaia:

[2] Grace to you and peace from God our Father and the Lord Jesus Christ.

[3] Blessed be the God and Father of our Lord Jesus Christ, the Father of mercies and God of all comfort, [4] who comforts us in all our tribulation, that we may be able to comfort those who are in any trouble, with the comfort with which we ourselves are comforted by God. [5] For as the sufferings of Christ abound in us, so our consolation also abounds through Christ. [6] Now if we are afflicted, it is for your consolation and salvation, which is effective for enduring the same sufferings which we also suffer. Or if we are comforted, it is for your consolation and salvation. [7] And our hope for you is steadfast, because we know that as you are partakers of the sufferings, so also you will partake of the consolation.

---

1. Paul opens by referring to himself as an *apostle* of Jesus Christ—an important point for him to make given that many in the church were questioning his authority. What praise does Paul then give to God? What does Paul say God is able to do for us (see verses 1–4)?

2. Paul and his coworkers had endured many trials for the sake of the gospel. How does Paul say that these afflictions had actually benefitted the believers (see verses 6–7)?

_____

_____

_____

_____

_____

_____

_____

_____

_____

_____

_____

_____

Delivered from Suffering (2 Corinthians 1:8–11)

[8] For we do not want you to be ignorant, brethren, of our trouble which came to us in Asia: that we were burdened beyond measure, above strength, so that we despaired even of life. [9] Yes, we had the sentence of death in ourselves, that we should not trust in ourselves but in God who raises the dead, [10] who delivered us from so great a death, and does deliver us; in whom we trust that He will still deliver us, [11] you also helping together in prayer for us, that thanks may be given by many persons on our behalf for the gift granted to us through many.

3. Paul's passing mention of the "affliction" that he and his fellow workers had endured indicates that the Corinthian believers already had knowledge of the event. What effect does Paul say that this episode had on himself and his companions (see verses 8–9)?

_____

_____

_____

_____

_____

4. What hope did Paul place in God in spite of this trial? What does he ask the Corinthian believers to do for him and his companions (see verses 10–11)?

_____

_____

_____

_____

_____

_____

_____

Paul Defends His Sincerity (2 Corinthians 1:12–14)

¹² For our boasting is this: the testimony of our conscience that we conducted ourselves in the world in simplicity and godly sincerity, not with fleshly wisdom but by the grace of God, and more abundantly toward you. ¹³ For we are not writing any other things to you than what you read or understand. Now I trust you will understand, even to the end ¹⁴ (as also you have understood us in part), that we are your boast as you also are ours, in the day of the Lord Jesus.

5. Paul's experience in Asia forced him to abandon any notions of self-reliance and trust completely in God for deliverance. How does Paul now describe his "boasting"? How was his ministry different from that of others who had come to Corinth (see verse 12)?

_____

_____

_____

_____

_____

_____

6. By this time, the believers in Corinth had received the letter we call 1 Corinthians and another "severe letter" letter from Paul (which is not known to us today.) What did Paul say about his intentions in writing these letters? What did he ask the believers to remember about his conduct (see verses 13–14)?

_____

_____

_____

_____

_____

_____

_____

Paul Defends His Change of Plans (2 Corinthians 1:15–24)

¹⁵ And in this confidence I intended to come to you before, that you might have a second benefit—¹⁶ to pass by way of you to Macedonia,

to come again from Macedonia to you, and be helped by you on my way to Judea. ¹⁷ Therefore, when I was planning this, did I do it lightly? Or the things I plan, do I plan according to the flesh, that with me there should be Yes, Yes, and No, No? ¹⁸ But as God is faithful, our word to you was not Yes and No. ¹⁹ For the Son of God, Jesus Christ, who was preached among you by us—by me, Silvanus, and Timothy—was not Yes and No, but in Him was Yes. ²⁰ For all the promises of God in Him are Yes, and in Him Amen, to the glory of God through us. ²¹ Now He who establishes us with you in Christ and has anointed us is God, ²² who also has sealed us and given us the Spirit in our hearts as a guarantee.

²³ Moreover I call God as witness against my soul, that to spare you I came no more to Corinth. ²⁴ Not that we have dominion over your faith, but are fellow workers for your joy; for by faith you stand.

---

7. Paul's critics had not only charged that he had acted in an insincere manner toward the Corinthians but also that he had deliberately altered his plans to visit them out of spite. How does Paul respond to these allegations (see verses 15–21)?

_____

_____

_____

_____

_____

_____

_____

_____

_____

_____

_____

_____

8. What additional reasons does Paul give for not coming to Corinth (see verses 23–24)?

_____

_____

_____

_____

_____

_____

_____

REVIEWING THE STORY

Paul began his letter to the Corinthian believers by stating that he and his coworkers had recently endured a time of "trouble" in Asia that made them despair for their lives. Paul said that he had to rely even more on God during this time and considered it a blessing if his sufferings led to the consolation and salvation of others. Paul's hope for the believers remained steadfast. The apostle then responded to accusations that he was insincere in his dealings with the Corinthians or was fickle and unreliable because of his change in travel plans. Paul reminded the believers that he had preached about a Jesus who was reliable and trustworthy—so how could he thus be anything less than sincere and trustworthy?

9. How did Paul identify himself in order to remind the Corinthian believers of his authority (see 2 Corinthians 1:1)?

_____

_____

_____

_____

_____

_____

_____

10. How did Paul respond to the death sentence hanging over his head in Asia (see 2 Corinthians 1:9)?

_____

_____

_____

_____

_____

_____

_____

_____

11. In what did Paul say that he boasted (see 2 Corinthians 1:12)?

_____

_____

_____

_____

_____

_____

_____

_____

12. What comment did Paul make to remind the Corinthian believers of his credentials as an apostle (see 2 Corinthians 1:21–22)?

_____

_____

_____

_____

_____

_____

_____

APPLYING THE MESSAGE

13. How would you respond to someone who accused you of being insincere or hypocritical in your Christian faith?

_____

_____

_____

_____

_____

_____

14. What would you say or do if you discovered that one of your closest Christian friends was being insincere or hypocritical in his or her faith?

_____

_____

_____

_____

_____

_____

REFLECTING ON THE MEANING

Paul was facing a threat in his relationship with the Corinthians. Members of the congregation were listening to the apostle's opponents, who stood to gain if his reputation took a hit. The believers were questioning Paul's sincerity and implying that his ministry to them had been motivated by something other than God's call. They were saying Paul was a hypocrite—one who holds others to a certain spiritual standard but ignores that standard himself.

Paul understood that his reputation was at stake, so he offered a carefully reasoned defense of his actions. Of course, he had the advantage of knowing that he *had* been sincere in his dealings with them—that he was operating from a position of innocence. Sadly, this is a luxury not all believers enjoy. Maintaining sincere and God-honoring interactions with others is a constant challenge. Many times, we open ourselves to criticism and accusations of being insincere or hypocritical. As was the case with Paul, if those criticisms and accusations follow us around, they can damage our reputation and our Christian witness and ministry.

There are three simple steps that we can take in our lives to protect or repair our reputation and maintain our spiritual sincerity. The first step is to *pray*. We commit our plans to God and ask Him to guard our hearts against insincerity. We ask Him to make us aware, through the prompting of the Holy Spirit, of past interactions in which we were less than sincere. This gives us the opportunity to seek out people we may have offended and make amends.

The second step is to *examine ourselves*. The roots of our insincerity could spring from a desire to be liked (saying things people want to hear) or a cavalier attitude toward making plans (agreeing to things without first checking schedules), or from a place of ignorance (being unaware of how others perceive us). Examining ourselves involves gathering input from others—people whose judgment we trust—so they can shine a light on areas in our lives that we cannot see. Of course, inviting scrutiny will require us to swallow our pride, and we will discover things about ourselves we do not like. But that information is necessary and valuable.

The third step is to place a *renewed emphasis on sincerity and integrity*. We do this in both big and small ways. We look for opportunities to sacrifice our time and energy for others. We practice what we preach. We do not commit to certain plans until we are sure we can fulfill the commitment. To paraphrase Jesus' words in Matthew 5:37, we let our yes be yes and our no be no. We commit to speaking the truth in love, even when the truth is hard for someone to hear. We build a reputation as someone whose walk with Christ is genuine and sincere.

JOURNALING YOUR RESPONSE

What are some areas in your life where you need to be more sincere?

IDENTIFIED WITH CHRIST

2 Corinthians 2:1–3:18

GETTING STARTED

What are some triumphs that you have personally experienced in your walk with God?

_____

_____

_____

_____

_____

_____

_____

_____

_____

_____

_____

_____

_____

_____

_____

_____

_____

SETTING THE STAGE

Letters of recommendation were vital for itinerant speakers in the first century. When a minister arrived in a new city, the people often based their decision on whether to offer hospitality to the speaker on his letter of recommendation. It wasn't just a matter of *what* you knew—it was also a matter of *who* you knew. A letter of recommendation from the right person could open all kinds of doors for you.

Not all speakers carried such letters. Paul, for his part, refused to carry such letters—a fact that his enemies used against him. Of course, by this time Paul should have been past the point of *needing* such letters. He had carried the gospel to more places than most people visit in a lifetime. He had endured countless beatings and attempts on his life. He had planted and nurtured more than a dozen churches—including the one in Corinth. He had financed his own ministry by making tents so he would not be indebted to any group or person. He was respected by other apostles. He had *written* letters of recommendation for other people.

But that did not stop Paul's critics from questioning his credentials and sowing seeds of distrust among the believers in Corinth. Many in the church were only too happy to water those seeds. Paul had bruised the Corinthians' egos with his previous letters. He had confronted them about their un-Christlike behavior and had made them face some harsh truths about themselves. So, questioning his credentials was a way for them to save face.

No one would have blamed Paul for being offended by the Corinthians' actions. But instead, he responded with humility. If the Corinthian believers wanted evidence for Paul's eligibility as a speaker and proclaimer of the gospel, he was only too glad to show them. His credentials came from the identity he received when he was transformed by Christ.

EXPLORING THE TEXT

Paul Urges Forgiveness (2 Corinthians 2:1–11)

[1] But I determined this within myself, that I would not come again to you in sorrow. [2] For if I make you sorrowful, then who is he who makes me glad but the one who is made sorrowful by me?

³ And I wrote this very thing to you, lest, when I came, I should have sorrow over those from whom I ought to have joy, having confidence in you all that my joy is the joy of you all. ⁴ For out of much affliction and anguish of heart I wrote to you, with many tears, not that you should be grieved, but that you might know the love which I have so abundantly for you.

⁵ But if anyone has caused grief, he has not grieved me, but all of you to some extent—not to be too severe. ⁶ This punishment which was inflicted by the majority is sufficient for such a man, ⁷ so that, on the contrary, you ought rather to forgive and comfort him, lest perhaps such a one be swallowed up with too much sorrow. ⁸ Therefore I urge you to reaffirm your love to him. ⁹ For to this end I also wrote, that I might put you to the test, whether you are obedient in all things. ¹⁰ Now whom you forgive anything, I also forgive. For if indeed I have forgiven anything, I have forgiven that one for your sakes in the presence of Christ, ¹¹ lest Satan should take advantage of us; for we are not ignorant of his devices.

1. Paul had determined that given the current situation, a visit to Corinth would have only led to further sorrow for himself and the congregation. So, he instead wrote a "severe" (or "sorrowful") letter to them in place of that visit. What was Paul's emotional state when he wrote this letter? What was his purpose in writing it (see verses 1–4)?

2. Paul was anguished about the accusations leveled against him, but he was not willing to retaliate against those who had caused him this grief. What does Paul say the church should do regarding the man who had wronged him? What does Paul state as his reason for forgiving the man—and urging the church to do likewise (see verses 5–11)?

_____

_____

_____

_____

_____

_____

_____

_____

_____

_____

Triumph in Christ (2 Corinthians 2:12–17)

¹² Furthermore, when I came to Troas to preach Christ's gospel, and a door was opened to me by the Lord, ¹³ I had no rest in my spirit, because I did not find Titus my brother; but taking my leave of them, I departed for Macedonia.

¹⁴ Now thanks be to God who always leads us in triumph in Christ, and through us diffuses the fragrance of His knowledge in every place. ¹⁵ For we are to God the fragrance of Christ among those who are being saved and among those who are perishing. ¹⁶ To the one we are the aroma of death leading to death, and to the other the aroma of life leading to life. And who is sufficient for these things? ¹⁷ For we are not, as so many, peddling the word of God; but as of sincerity, but as from God, we speak in the sight of God in Christ.

3. What further reason does Paul provide for choosing not to visit Corinth (see verses 12–13)?

_____

_____

_____

_____

_____

_____

_____

4. The memories of Paul's reunion with Titus in Macedonia prompts him to begin a "great digression" about the apostolic ministry. How does Paul describe his work as a minister of the gospel? How is he different from other itinerant speakers (see verses 14–17)?

_____

_____

_____

_____

_____

_____

_____

Christ's Epistle (2 Corinthians 3:1–6)

¹ Do we begin again to commend ourselves? Or do we need, as some others, epistles of commendation to you or letters of commendation from you? ² You are our epistle written in our hearts, known and read by all men; ³ clearly you are an epistle of Christ, ministered by us, written not with ink but by the Spirit of the living God, not on tablets of stone but on tablets of flesh, that is, of the heart.

⁴ And we have such trust through Christ toward God. ⁵ Not that we are sufficient of ourselves to think of anything as being from

ourselves, but our sufficiency is from God, ⁶ who also made us sufficient as ministers of the new covenant, not of the letter but of the Spirit; for the letter kills, but the Spirit gives life.

---

5. Paul poses two questions to the believers in Corinth . . . each with an expected answer of "no." What do these questions reveal about the charges that had been levelled against Paul? What does Paul say was the "proof" of his ministry among them (see verses 1–3)?

_____

_____

_____

_____

_____

_____

6. In what did Paul say that he placed his trust? What did the apostle add to emphasize that he was not taking credit for the transformation in the believers' lives (see verses 4–5)?

_____

_____

_____

_____

_____

_____

The Glory of the New Covenant (2 Corinthians 3:7–18)

⁷ But if the ministry of death, written and engraved on stones, was glorious, so that the children of Israel could not look steadily at the face of Moses because of the glory of his countenance, which glory

was passing away, [8] how will the ministry of the Spirit not be more glorious? [9] For if the ministry of condemnation had glory, the ministry of righteousness exceeds much more in glory. [10] For even what was made glorious had no glory in this respect, because of the glory that excels. [11] For if what is passing away was glorious, what remains is much more glorious.

[12] Therefore, since we have such hope, we use great boldness of speech—[13] unlike Moses, who put a veil over his face so that the children of Israel could not look steadily at the end of what was passing away. [14] But their minds were blinded. For until this day the same veil remains unlifted in the reading of the Old Testament, because the veil is taken away in Christ. [15] But even to this day, when Moses is read, a veil lies on their heart. [16] Nevertheless when one turns to the Lord, the veil is taken away. [17] Now the Lord is the Spirit; and where the Spirit of the Lord is, there is liberty. [18] But we all, with unveiled face, beholding as in a mirror the glory of the Lord, are being transformed into the same image from glory to glory, just as by the Spirit of the Lord.

---

7. Paul's mention of his work as a minister "of the new covenant" causes him to reflect on the differences between the old and new covenants. How does Paul refer to the old covenant? How does he describe the blessings of the new covenant (see verses 7–11)?

8. Paul notes that Moses placed a veil over his face after he met with God so the Israelites would not be dazzled by the radiance of the Lord that remained on him (see Exodus 34:33–35). How does Paul use this imagery to point out the differences between those who are still under the burden of the law and those who are in Christ (see 2 Corinthians 3:12–18)?

_____

_____

_____

_____

_____

_____

_____

_____

_____

REVIEWING THE STORY

Paul continued to defend his ministry among the Corinthians by stating that he changed his travel plans in order to avoid pain for both himself and the believers. He explained that he had chosen to instead write a heartfelt letter to them so they would understand the love he had for them. Paul then encouraged the church to forgive a man who had evidently stirred up trouble against him, noting that such forgiveness would allow them to thwart Satan's plans to create division in the church. Following this, Paul began a digression in which he pointed to the Corinthian believers as his "letter of recommendation" and identified himself as one of the ministers of the new covenant. He compared this new covenant of Jesus with the old covenant of the law and pointed out the liberty and transforming glory that the new covenant had brought.

9. What did Paul want to communicate to the Corinthians in his letter (see 2 Corinthians 2:4)?

_____

_____

_____

_____

10. How did God direct the apostle Paul's ministry in the city of Troas (see 2 Corinthians 2:12)?

_____

_____

_____

_____

11. Why did Paul describe the Corinthian believers as "an epistle of Christ" (see 2 Corinthians 3:1–3)?

_____

_____

_____

_____

12. What are Christ's followers able to do because of the hope of the new covenant (see 2 Corinthians 3:12)?

_____

_____

_____

_____

_____

APPLYING THE MESSAGE

13. Why is it so important to forgive those who have sought to do wrong against you?

_____

_____

_____

_____

_____

_____

_____

_____

14. In what ways has God given you boldness to spread the message of Jesus Christ?

_____

_____

_____

_____

_____

_____

_____

_____

REFLECTING ON THE MEANING

In this section of the letter, Paul writes that one reason he had not returned to Corinth was because God had opened a door to a different ministry opportunity (see 2 Corinthians 2:12–13). Paul's close relationship with

God enabled him to discern the Lord's will and walk obediently through the doors that He had opened. Today, we can follow Paul's example and also learn how to discern God's guidance by incorporating a few important disciplines into our lives.

First, we need to have *daily communication with the Lord*. If we want to recognize the Holy Spirit's leading in our lives, we need to have constant fellowship with Him. This starts with a daily quiet time that includes Bible study, prayer, and—perhaps most essentially for the purposes of this discussion—listening time. God speaks to us through the prompting of His Holy Spirit. If we listen carefully, blocking out the noise and distractions of daily life, we will get a sense of where He is leading us next.

Second, we need to incorporate *flexibility into our lives*. An old Yiddish proverb says, "Man plans, and God laughs." Our power to predict the future—even our *own* future—is quite limited. We cannot trust or assume that our lives will follow a predictable pattern. Rather, we need to be ready and prepared for the unpredictable to happen. Every day is a new day with God—a day rife with potential for change. We can either deny that potential or embrace it.

Third, we need a *seasoned faith*. We need to be able to recognize the goodness that God has bestowed on us and acknowledge that He has our best interests in mind. As we walk with God, we come to realize how He uses even difficult situations in our lives to help us grow in our faith and learn to trust in Him. We come to understand why certain doors were opened to us and others were closed. When we can trace this pattern and see that God did all of this for our benefit, we can trust that He will do the same in every situation we face.

Fourth, we need *a spirit of adventure*. When God opens a door, it is often an exit from our comfort zone. We have no way of knowing where it will lead or what lies beyond—but we do know that we can trust the One who opened the door. So we can step through it with a sense of expectation, knowing that something incredible lies ahead. As Paul concluded, "Now thanks be to God who always leads us in triumph in Christ" (2 Corinthians 2:14).

JOURNALING YOUR RESPONSE

What are some doors that God has opened and closed in your life?

TREASURE IN EARTHEN VESSELS

2 Corinthians 4:1–18

GETTING STARTED

What is a failure in your life that you have worked hard to overcome?

SETTING THE STAGE

As Paul writes in this next section, our bodies are "earthen vessels" and "we are hard-pressed on every side" (2 Corinthians 4:7–8). Yet Jesus has shared the incredible light of His gospel with us and commissioned us to share it with others. As His disciples, we have been entrusted with the most important message of all time.

The Corinthians had put the messenger who had brought this gospel message to them under scrutiny. They had analyzed his approach, his speaking style, and even his personal characteristics and had concluded there was nothing at all remarkable about him. If his message was truly sent by God, shouldn't there have been something more *special* about him?

Paul's response is that the believers were missing the point. It is *exactly* because the message is so important that the messenger is so weak. Just like a treasure in an earthen vessel, it is not the fragile, breakable, disposable vessel that matters most but the treasure it carries inside. If that were not the case, the vessel might think it was the treasure! The life of the disciple must be modeled on the gospel itself.

Paul stresses that to see the truth of the resurrection at work in our lives, we must be prepared to see the crucifixion at work as well. At times, like the apostle Paul, we will feel hard-pressed, perplexed, persecuted, and struck down (see verses 8–9). However, when we belong to Christ, we can be assured that we will not be crushed, left in despair, forsaken, or destroyed. This should serve as an incredible comfort to us all. We are indeed "earthen vessels" on this earth, but we carry within us the treasure of the light of the gospel.

EXPLORING THE TEXT

The Light of Christ's Gospel (2 Corinthians 4:1–6)

¹ Therefore, since we have this ministry, as we have received mercy, we do not lose heart. ² But we have renounced the hidden things

of shame, not walking in craftiness nor handling the word of God deceitfully, but by manifestation of the truth commending ourselves to every man's conscience in the sight of God. ³ But even if our gospel is veiled, it is veiled to those who are perishing, ⁴ whose minds the god of this age has blinded, who do not believe, lest the light of the gospel of the glory of Christ, who is the image of God, should shine on them. ⁵ For we do not preach ourselves, but Christ Jesus the Lord, and ourselves your bondservants for Jesus' sake. ⁶ For it is the God who commanded light to shine out of darkness, who has shone in our hearts to give the light of the knowledge of the glory of God in the face of Jesus Christ.

---

1. The apostle Paul has just discussed the benefits of the new covenant and what it means for believers in Christ. He now returns to discussing his role as a minister of that new covenant. Why does Paul say that he has no reason to lose heart in spite of the trials he faced? What does Paul state that he has renounced (see verses 1–2)?

2. Some had claimed that Paul's gospel was obscure and that his methods were under-handed. How does Paul respond to these charges? What does he say is really happening if people are not able to see the truth of the gospel he proclaims (see verses 3–6)?

_____

_____

_____

_____

_____

_____

_____

_____

_____

_____

_____

_____

_____

_____

Paradoxes of the Faith (2 Corinthians 4:7–12)

7 But we have this treasure in earthen vessels, that the excellence of the power may be of God and not of us. 8 We are hard-pressed on every side, yet not crushed; we are perplexed, but not in despair; 9 persecuted, but not forsaken; struck down, but not destroyed— 10 always carrying about in the body the dying of the Lord Jesus, that the life of Jesus also may be manifested in our body. 11 For we who live are always delivered to death for Jesus' sake, that the life of Jesus also may be manifested in our mortal flesh. 12 So then death is working in us, but life in you.

3. Why does Paul say that God entrusted the "treasure" of the gospel to an "earthen vessel" like himself (see verse 7)?

_____

_____

_____

_____

_____

_____

4. What paradoxes of the Christian life does Paul highlight in verses 8–9? What was Paul willing to endure so the message of salvation could reach the lost (see verses 11–12)?

_____

_____

_____

_____

_____

_____

_____

_____

Compelled to Spread the Gospel (2 Corinthians 4:13–15)

¹³ And since we have the same spirit of faith, according to what is written, "I believed and therefore I spoke," we also believe and therefore speak, ¹⁴ knowing that He who raised up the Lord Jesus will also raise us up with Jesus, and will present us with you. ¹⁵ For all things are for your sakes, that grace, having spread through the many, may cause thanksgiving to abound to the glory of God.

5. Paul quotes the psalmist who wrote, "I believe, therefore I spoke, I am greatly afflicted" (Psalm 116:10). Why couldn't Paul remain silent about Christ (see 1 Corinthians 4:13–14)?

_____

_____

_____

_____

_____

_____

_____

_____

_____

_____

6. How does Paul conclude his argument that he was sincere in his ministry to the Corinthians? What had he endured for their sake (see verse 15)?

_____

_____

_____

_____

_____

_____

_____

_____

_____

_____

_____

_____

_____

Seeing the Invisible (2 Corinthians 4:16–18)

¹⁶ Therefore we do not lose heart. Even though our outward man is perishing, yet the inward man is being renewed day by day. ¹⁷ For our light affliction, which is but for a moment, is working for us a far more exceeding and eternal weight of glory, ¹⁸ while we do not look at the things which are seen, but at the things which are not seen. For the things which are seen are temporary, but the things which are not seen are eternal.

7. The trials that Paul had endured took their toll on his physical health. But why did he refuse to lose heart even in the face of this fact (see verse 16)?

8. How did the apostle Paul consider his trials in this world? How did his perspective enable him to continue his ministry to reveal the "unseen" truths of the gospel (see verses 17–18)?

_____

_____

_____

_____

_____

_____

_____

REVIEWING THE STORY

Paul shed light on the inner workings of his ministry by discussing how he presented the glorious new covenant to the lost. He explained to the Corinthians that he had preached the gospel of Christ with boldness, humility, honesty, and integrity. He pointed out that people who choose not to respond to such a glorious message have been spiritually blinded by Satan. Paul emphasized that he preached Jesus—not himself—and noted that it was the power of the gospel within him that proved his sincerity and integrity. He noted how his own suffering had served to bring spiritual riches to others and encouraged the believers to not lose heart.

9. What title did Paul use to refer to Satan (see 2 Corinthians 4:4)?

_____

_____

_____

_____

_____

_____

10. How did Paul describe the impact of the difficulties he faced (see 2 Corinthians 4:8–9)?

_____

_____

_____

_____

_____

_____

_____

11. What does Paul say empowers us to speak the message of Christ (see 2 Corinthians 4:13–14)?

_____

_____

_____

_____

_____

_____

_____

12. What is the essential difference between the things that are seen and the things that are not seen (see 2 Corinthians 4:18)?

_____

_____

_____

_____

_____

_____

_____

APPLYING THE MESSAGE

13. What are some ways that you are "hard-pressed" on every side? What encouragement can you take from Paul's outlook on the trials we all endure in life?

_____

_____

_____

_____

_____

_____

_____

14. What are some ways that you keep your focus on the promise of eternity with Christ? How does this help you to endure the *momentary* afflictions in this life?

_____

_____

_____

_____

_____

_____

_____

REFLECTING ON THE MEANING

It is easy to lose heart when you face trials, setbacks, and failures. But failures in life do not need to define you. Rather, you are defined by your God-given identity of disciple. As long as you remain in Him, you continue to be defined by Him, not by any failings. So how do you remain in Christ though you are still an "earthen vessel" that makes mistakes?

First, *admit your mistakes*. Your primary instinct will be to downplay the failure, but instead choose to be honest about who you are. Failing to admit your mistakes will create false illusions for yourself and those who know you. If people are going to recognize God's work in your life, they have to see the work of Christ in you in both the ups *and* the downs.

Second, *accept God's forgiveness* if your failure involves sin. The only way to overcome sin is to ask God to forgive you—and then embrace the forgiveness that He offers. As David wrote, "He has not dealt with us according to our sins, nor punished us according to our iniquities" (Psalm 103:10). God specializes in forgiving failures. There is nothing you have done that cannot be forgiven if you come to God in repentance. Once you have asked for God's forgiveness, receive it. It is a gift of grace that you cannot earn.

Third, *apply the lessons you learned in failure toward success*. Author John Keats wrote, "Failure is, in a sense, the highway to success, inasmuch as every discovery of what is false leads us to seek earnestly after what is true, and every fresh experience points out some form of error which we shall afterwards carefully avoid." Don't throw your failures away. Use them to learn how to more fully trust Christ and succeed by His power and ability. God will often allow your failures to become distinctive points of power and ministry in your life.

Fourth, *accept failure as a* fact *of life, not as a* way *of life*. Failure is something that happens because of bad choices. It is not our identity. Peter is an excellent illustration of this point. When he denied Jesus, he failed three different times . . . one right after the other. Yet it was not long before he delivered one of the most powerful sermons ever preached on the Day of Pentecost. The only way to explain this transformation is Peter's encounter with the risen Christ and the power of the Holy Spirit in his life. Jesus forgave this "earthen vessel" and equipped Peter to carry the light of His gospel to the world.

Finally, *arise from failure and start again*. When you fail, don't feel sorry for yourself and wallow in self-pity. God loves you and has chosen you as a vessel to carry His gift to the world. He doesn't make bad decisions. So get back on your feet and get started moving forward again.

JOURNALING YOUR RESPONSE

When you think of your most recent failure, where are you on the list of the five things to do?

LESSON *four*

THE GOSPEL OF RECONCILIATION

2 Corinthians 5:1–21

GETTING STARTED

What is the longest you have ever been estranged from a loved one?

_____

_____

_____

_____

_____

_____

_____

_____

_____

_____

_____

_____

_____

_____

_____

SETTING THE STAGE

When a couple is contemplating a divorce, one of the questions a marriage counselor will ask is whether there is any hope for reconciliation. In other words, is there anything that can be done to prevent the two sides from separating for good? This same question lies at the heart of our relationship with God. As Paul wrote in his letter to the Romans, "All have sinned and fall short of the glory of God" (3:23). We are *all* estranged from God and need to be reconciled.

As previously noted, the believers in Corinth had a high opinion of themselves. So Paul first needed to help them see that they were the cause of the estrangement. The same is true for us. No matter how kind, good, loving, unselfish, or caring we might be, we have committed sins against God that have severed our relationship with him. Our sins have created a gulf between us and a holy God. We have all fallen short of God's glory.

The question then becomes whether there is anything that can be done to restore the relationship. The answer, as Paul will show in this next section of his letter to the Corinthians, is that there is nothing we can do on our own to correct the problem. However, when we choose to believe in Christ, we are "a new creation; old things have passed away; behold, all things have become new." God alone "has reconciled us to Himself through Jesus Christ" (2 Corinthians 5:17–18). God's love for us was so great that He was willing to sacrifice His only Son to restore our fellowship. This is the "good news" of the gospel.

Our part then becomes to receive the good news. John wrote, "For God so loved the world that He gave His only begotten Son, that whoever *believes in Him* should not perish but have everlasting life" (John 3:16, emphasis added). We believe in Jesus and acknowledge that He has paid the price that God demanded for our sins. We repent of our sins and accept the sacrifice that Christ made for us on the cross. We believe that God has restored our fellowship and choose to walk in His ways.

Jesus alone makes our reconciliation with God possible. But what a reconciliation it is! Because of Jesus' sacrifice, we are "holy, and blameless, and above reproach in His sight" (Colossians 1:22). We become worthy to spend eternity in God's presence.

EXPLORING THE TEXT

Assurance of the Resurrection (2 Corinthians 5:1–8)

[1] For we know that if our earthly house, this tent, is destroyed, we have a building from God, a house not made with hands, eternal in the heavens. [2] For in this we groan, earnestly desiring to be clothed with our habitation which is from heaven, [3] if indeed, having been clothed, we shall not be found naked. [4] For we who are in this tent groan, being burdened, not because we want to be unclothed, but further clothed, that mortality may be swallowed up by life. [5] Now He who has prepared us for this very thing is God, who also has given us the Spirit as a guarantee.

[6] So we are always confident, knowing that while we are at home in the body we are absent from the Lord. [7] For we walk by faith, not by sight. [8] We are confident, yes, well pleased rather to be absent from the body and to be present with the Lord.

1. Paul has just noted that even in the midst of affliction, perplexity, persecution—and in the face of death—believers are able to hold on to the hope they have received through Christ. To what hope can we cling if our "earthly house" (our body) is destroyed (see verse 1)?

2. How does keeping our focus on eternity help us to navigate the trials of this world? How does this require walking by faith and not by sight (see verses 4–7)?

_____

_____

_____

_____

_____

_____

_____

_____

_____

_____

_____

_____

_____

_____

_____

_____

_____

_____

The Judgment Seat of Christ (2 Corinthians 5:9–11)

⁹ Therefore we make it our aim, whether present or absent, to be well pleasing to Him. ¹⁰ For we must all appear before the judgment seat of Christ, that each one may receive the things done in the body, according to what he has done, whether good or bad. ¹¹ Knowing, therefore, the terror of the Lord, we persuade men; but we are well known to God, and I also trust are well known in your consciences.

3. Paul follows up his discussion on the hope we have received with some practical takeaways on how these truths should affect our lives. How does Paul say we should conduct ourselves? What should we remember as we consider our actions (see verses 9–10?)

_____

_____

_____

_____

_____

_____

_____

_____

_____

4. When Paul says we should know the "terror of the Lord," he is saying we should hold Him in reverential awe as the future judge of the world. How should this truth compel us to tell others about the gospel (see verse 11)?

_____

_____

_____

_____

_____

_____

_____

_____

_____

Compelled by Christ's Love (2 Corinthians 5:12–15)

> [12] For we do not commend ourselves again to you, but give you opportunity to boast on our behalf, that you may have an answer for those who boast in appearance and not in heart. [13] For if we are beside ourselves, it is for God; or if we are of sound mind, it is for you. [14] For the love of Christ compels us, because we judge thus: that if One died for all, then all died; [15] and He died for all, that those who live should live no longer for themselves, but for Him who died for them and rose again.

5. Paul again returns to the defense of his ministry when he was with the Corinthians. In what does he want the believers to "boast" (see verse 12)?

6. What does Paul say motivated all his actions? How does he say that we should live in light of knowing the truth that Jesus died for our sins (see verses 13–15)?

_____

_____

_____

_____

_____

_____

_____

_____

_____

_____

_____

_____

Be Reconciled to God (2 Corinthians 5:16–21)

16 Therefore, from now on, we regard no one according to the flesh. Even though we have known Christ according to the flesh, yet now we know Him thus no longer. 17 Therefore, if anyone is in Christ, he is a new creation; old things have passed away; behold, all things have become new. 18 Now all things are of God, who has reconciled us to Himself through Jesus Christ, and has given us the ministry of reconciliation, 19 that is, that God was in Christ reconciling the world to Himself, not imputing their trespasses to them, and has committed to us the word of reconciliation.

20 Now then, we are ambassadors for Christ, as though God were pleading through us: we implore you on Christ's behalf, be reconciled to God. 21 For He made Him who knew no sin to be sin for us, that we might become the righteousness of God in Him.

7. Paul had learned to not judge people in terms of "the flesh" or outward appearances but on the spiritual condition of their hearts. What does Paul say about a person who has received Christ? What changes have taken place in that person's life (see verses 16–17)?

8. Paul states that it was God who reached out to sinful humankind and made the initial steps toward restoration. What task has He given to us in this respect? In what ways are we to be "ambassadors for Christ" (see verses 18–21)?

REVIEWING THE STORY

Paul stated that as believers, we have a heavenly body and an eternal home waiting for us at the end of this life. We can therefore live with confidence, knowing what our future holds. In light of this truth, our aim should thus be to please God in this life. Paul then again defended his ministry to the Corinthians, emphasizing that he was not crazy (as some of the believers evidently suspected) but simply motivated by the love that he received from the Lord. Paul explained that he no longer regarded anyone from a worldly point of view but only from the spiritual condition of their hearts. He urged the believers to accept the work that Jesus was doing in their lives and partner with him in spreading the message of the gospel.

9. What reason does Paul give as to why Christians "groan" in this present world (see 2 Corinthians 5:2)?

_____

_____

_____

_____

_____

_____

10. What will happen when we appear before the judgment seat of Christ (see 2 Corinthians 5:10)?

_____

_____

_____

_____

_____

_____

_____

11. Whom does Paul say was able to impress the Corinthian Christians (see 2 Corinthians 5:12)?

_____

_____

_____

_____

12. What is true of anyone who is in Christ (see 2 Corinthians 5:17)?

_____

_____

_____

APPLYING THE MESSAGE

13. How would you explain to an unbeliever what happens when you stop living for yourself and start living for Christ?

_____

_____

_____

_____

_____

14. How can you prevent yourself from becoming overly impressed by people who "boast in appearance and not in heart" (2 Corinthians 5:12)?

_____

_____

_____

_____

REFLECTING ON THE MEANING

In this section of Paul's letter, he uses a political analogy to help the Corinthian believers—and us—understand the responsibilities of being a Christian. Paul wrote, "We are ambassadors for Christ" (5:20). This analogy carries the following profound implications for our lives.

First, *as Christ's ambassadors we no longer represent ourselves.* As God's representatives, we do not have the freedom to indulge our own desires. Everything we now do is to bring honor to God. We represent God not only in an "official" capacity but also in every aspect of life. Everything about us—the company we keep, the entertainment we choose, the way we treat our bodies, the way we interact with others, the priorities we set—reflects Him. There are no off-hours for ambassadors for Christ.

Second, *as Christ's ambassadors we have a code of conduct to uphold.* In the political realm, ambassadors are expected to follow a certain protocol. In the Christian realm, we are held to an even higher standard. Many of our responsibilities as ambassadors are clearly spelled out for us in God's Word. They can be found everywhere from the life lessons of Proverbs to the words of Jesus in His Sermon on the Mount to the exhortations of Paul.

Third, *as Christ's ambassadors we have been selected for our specific appointments.* God is the One who recognizes our gifts and abilities and appoints us to certain duties in service to His kingdom. His assignments allow us to use our gifts and abilities and put them to work. We are also empowered to carry out His purposes through the power of the Holy Spirit.

Finally, as *Christ's ambassadors we are on temporary assignment.* Like political ambassadors, we have a temporary dwelling place in a foreign land and will be called home one day. In the meantime, while we may speak the same language as locals, we do not share their same priorities or motivations. Instead, we represent Christ and His kingdom as we diligently act as agents of reconciliation in this broken world. If we do this faithfully, we can anticipate that when our tour of duty comes to an end, the One who appointed us will welcome us home with the words, "Well done, good and faithful servant" (Matthew 25:21).

JOURNALING YOUR RESPONSE

What is the most challenging aspect of being an ambassador for Christ?

LESSON *five*

UNEQUALLY YOKED

2 Corinthians 6:1–18

GETTING STARTED

How are your relationships with Christian friends different from your relationships with non-Christian friends?

SETTING THE STAGE

The believers in Corinth had been receptive to the message of the gospel. Paul considered them as brothers and sisters and fellow ambassadors for Christ. Yet he knew that the Corinthians had taken a troubling approach to their faith. They tolerated sexual immorality in their congregation and flirted with idolatry. They were swayed by intellectualism, which made them easy targets for smooth-talking false apostles looking for financial support. Some had evidently even begun to despise Paul for his plain-spoken wisdom and his refusal to accept money from them.

But perhaps the most troubling aspect for Paul was the Corinthians' refusal to distance themselves from the immoral influence of their culture. Corinth was home to a pagan temple whose priestesses served as prostitutes. The believers embraced the Corinthian culture and allowed it to permeate their congregation. The Corinthians seem to have embraced an impact-free form of Christianity. They identified themselves as Christ-followers but lived in a way that contradicted their beliefs. As a result, their witness was compromised.

This was an issue that Paul could not let slide. So, in this next section of his letter, he confronts the believers about the way they had embraced Corinth's immoral culture and maintained bonds with their pagan neighbors. He calls the Corinthians to a more impactful approach to Christianity—one that would require no small amount of sacrifice. He urges them to restructure their priorities so they will more closely align with God's. He also offers his own life as an example for the Corinthian Christians to follow.

To this end, Paul gives the believers a vivid description of what genuine faith looks like when it is put into action. His was a life that embodied patience and the ability to endure tribulations, needs, distress, and suffering. He tells of the hard work, the sleepless nights, the hunger, and the stress that went hand in hand with his own ministry. But he also speaks of the God-given resources he received that enabled him to accomplish his work.

Paul doesn't offer up the example of his life to boast about himself. Rather, he offers it to help the Corinthians recognize just how far their idea of Christianity was from reality.

EXPLORING THE TEXT

The Day of Salvation (2 Corinthians 6:1–2)

¹ We then, as workers together with Him also plead with you not to receive the grace of God in vain. ² For He says:

> "In an acceptable time I have heard you,
> And in the day of salvation I have helped you."

> Behold, now is the accepted time; behold, now is the day of salvation.

1. Paul considered himself to be a "worker" with God in not only spreading the message of Christ to non-believers but also in helping believers to live the way that God wanted them to live. In this regard, how could believers "receive the grace of God in vain" (see verse 1)?

2. Paul quotes from Isaiah 49:8. What does Paul say about the "day of salvation" (see verse 2)?

_____

_____

_____

_____

_____

_____

_____

_____

_____

_____

_____

_____

Marks of the Ministry (2 Corinthians 6:3–10)

³ We give no offense in anything, that our ministry may not be blamed. ⁴ But in all things we commend ourselves as ministers of God: in much patience, in tribulations, in needs, in distresses, ⁵ in stripes, in imprisonments, in tumults, in labors, in sleeplessness, in fastings; ⁶ by purity, by knowledge, by longsuffering, by kindness, by the Holy Spirit, by sincere love, ⁷ by the word of truth, by the power of God, by the armor of righteousness on the right hand and on the left, ⁸ by honor and dishonor, by evil report and good report; as deceivers, and yet true; ⁹ as unknown, and yet well known; as dying, and behold we live; as chastened, and yet not killed; ¹⁰ as sorrowful, yet always rejoicing; as poor, yet making many rich; as having nothing, and yet possessing all things.

3. Paul shows that the way he has lived his life testifies to his sincerity in bringing the gospel to the Corinthians. What are some of the positive traits that Paul lists that reveals what it means to be a true minister of the gospel (see verses 3–10)?

_____

_____

_____

_____

_____

_____

_____

_____

4. What are some of the struggles that Paul lists that reveals what a true minister of the gospel will be forced to endure at times?

_____

_____

_____

_____

_____

_____

_____

_____

Unequally Yoked (2 Corinthians 6:11–15)

[11] O Corinthians! We have spoken openly to you, our heart is wide open. [12] You are not restricted by us, but you are restricted by your own affections. [13] Now in return for the same (I speak as to children), you also be open.

¹⁴ Do not be unequally yoked together with unbelievers. For what fellowship has righteousness with lawlessness? And what communion has light with darkness? ¹⁵ And what accord has Christ with Belial? Or what part has a believer with an unbeliever?

---

5. Paul passionately exclaimed to the believers in Corinth that he had opened his heart and his life to them. What did he request in return (see verses 11–13)?

_____

_____

_____

_____

_____

_____

_____

_____

6. Paul desires for the believers to reciprocate his affections, but he knows there are barriers that stand in the way. What does he imply these barriers were? What is Paul calling to the believers' attention through the four questions he asks (see verses 14–15)?

_____

_____

_____

_____

_____

_____

_____

_____

_____

The Temple of God (2 Corinthians 6:16–18)

[16] And what agreement has the temple of God with idols? For you are the temple of the living God. As God has said:

> "I will dwell in them
> And walk among them.
> I will be their God,
> And they shall be My people."

[17] Therefore

> "Come out from among them
> And be separate, says the Lord.
> Do not touch what is unclean,
> And I will receive you."
> [18] "I will be a Father to you,
> And you shall be My sons and daughters,
> Says the Lord Almighty."

7. Paul now comes to the heart of the matter as to why believers should not enter into compromising relationships with non-believers. What do you think it means to be a "temple of the living God" (see verse 16)?

_____

_____

_____

_____

_____

_____

_____

_____

_____

8. According to Paul's quotation from Isaiah 52:11, what did God say His people had to do as a result of His dwelling with them? What did He promise in return (see verses 17–18)?

_____

_____

_____

_____

_____

_____

Reviewing the Story

Paul presented his résumé to the Corinthian Christians to prove his integrity and show what it means to be a follower of Christ and minister of the gospel. He presented himself as a coworker of Jesus—someone who was given a responsibility by God Himself. This responsibility had ignited a passion in him to be blameless as a servant of the gospel. Paul then called the believers to not be yoked with unbelievers or be persuaded by the ways of the world. He stated that he had been open and honest with them, that he desired for them to reciprocate his feelings, and that he wanted above all to be reconciled with them.

9. What was the apostle Paul able to confidently say about his ministry (see 2 Corinthians 6:3)?

_____

_____

_____

_____

_____

_____

10. What did Paul say that he was able to do even though he was poor (see 2 Corinthians 6:10)?

11. What was it that restricted the Corinthian Christians from embracing Paul (see 2 Corinthians 6:12)?

12. How did Paul want the Corinthian believers to think of themselves (see 2 Corinthians 6:16)?

APPLYING THE MESSAGE

13. What is the difference between the way other people see you and the way God sees you?

_____

_____

_____

_____

_____

_____

_____

_____

_____

_____

14. How would you know if you were unequally yoked with an unbeliever?

_____

_____

_____

_____

_____

_____

_____

_____

_____

_____

_____

REFLECTING ON THE MEANING

In Paul's instruction to "not be unequally yoked with unbelievers," he established a fine line for believers today. The Great Commission dictates that we spend time among unbelievers (see Matthew 28:16–20), which means building personal relationships with them. But at the same time, we need to be careful these relationships do not lead to us being negatively influenced to do things that are against our Christian principles.

To this end, there are three ways we can make sure our good habits will not be corrupted. The first is to *establish and maintain clear boundaries*. We should empathize with people's struggles, share our own, and speak the truth in love. We should meet people where they are—but this cannot jeopardize our own spiritual wellbeing or put us in a compromising position. Our job is to show others the difference Jesus makes in our lives. If we give in to the same temptations as the people we are trying to reach, we will send the opposite message from what God intends. This is why we must make sure that our position is clear.

Second, *we have to monitor the direction of influence in our relationships with unbelievers*. Sometimes we may convince ourselves that we are the ones exerting the influence when, in reality, it is we who are being influenced. The influence occurs so subtly that we do not even realize it. To avoid this problem, we need to recruit mature Christians who will help us monitor our interactions with unbelievers. Ideal accountability partners will be those who know us well, see us in a variety of settings, are able to recognize subtle shifts in our attitudes and behaviors, and will not hesitate to confront us about them.

Third, *we need to evangelize our relationships*. When evangelism is a top priority in our lives, we look for opportunities to share the life-changing potential of Christ. We engage sincerely with others. We empathize with their struggles. We identify their objections to the gospel and look for new ways to present it. More than anything else, we take the words of the apostle Peter to heart: "Always be ready to give a defense to everyone who asks you a reason for the hope that is in you" (1 Peter 3:15).

JOURNALING YOUR RESPONSE

What are some ways you can make sure you are maintaining spiritually healthy relationships with unbelievers?

LESSON *six*

SPEAKING THE TRUTH IN LOVE

2 Corinthians 7:1–16

GETTING STARTED

What are some ways that people have spoken "the truth in love" to you?

_____

_____

_____

_____

_____

_____

_____

_____

_____

_____

_____

_____

_____

_____

_____

_____

SETTING THE STAGE

We all have "blind spots" in our lives where we cannot see—or do not want to believe—the truth about ourselves.

Some of our blind spots are caused by our vanity. We refuse to acknowledge the truth about ourselves, even though it is apparent to everyone else in our lives. Some of our blind spots are caused by pride. We convince ourselves that we are knowledgeable or skilled in certain areas when we actually are not. Some of our blind spots are caused by willful ignorance. We do not want to know the truth because we are afraid it might constrain us or ruin our fun.

The believers in the city of Corinth had many spiritual blind spots . . . issues that the apostle Paul knew he needed to call to their attention in love so that their vision could be corrected. As previously noted, the apostle wrote the letter we know as 1 Corinthians to point out certain problems in the church, address questions the believers had, and admonish and encourage them to live according to the principles they had been taught. The believers had generally accepted this advice and taken steps to put it into practice.

But then . . . opponents of Paul arrived on the scene and called his sincerity, integrity, and motives into question. As a result, many of Paul's former friends in the Corinthian church were now rejecting him and questioning his authority. Paul was saddened by this reaction—but he did not allow it to deter him. He did not change his approach in ministering to the Corinthians or recant any of his previous statements. Rather, he drafted what is referred to as the "severe" or "sorrowful" letter to point out how the believers had been blinded to the truth.

In this section of 2 Corinthians, Paul recounts the joy that he experienced when he learned from his coworker Titus that the believers in the city had taken his letter to heart. As painful as it had been for him to write those words, it appears that it had all been worth it. The believers in Corinth still liked and respected Paul . . . which was a good step toward their reconciliation.

EXPLORING THE TEXT

A Renewed Appeal (2 Corinthians 7:1–4)

¹ Therefore, having these promises, beloved, let us cleanse ourselves from all filthiness of the flesh and spirit, perfecting holiness in the fear of God.

² Open your hearts to us. We have wronged no one, we have corrupted no one, we have cheated no one. ³ I do not say this to condemn; for I have said before that you are in our hearts, to die together and to live together. ⁴ Great is my boldness of speech toward you, great is my boasting on your behalf. I am filled with comfort. I am exceedingly joyful in all our tribulation.

1. Paul opens this section by reminding the believers of the promises that he has just cited from the Old Testament (see 6:16–18). How should the believers live in light of having received all these promises from God (see verse 1)?

_____

_____

_____

_____

_____

_____

_____

_____

_____

_____

_____

2. Paul renews his appeal for the believers to open their hearts to him. What defense does he offer here for his actions? How does Paul describe the intent behind all of the words, sermons, and teachings that he had given to them (see verses 2–4)?

_____

_____

_____

_____

_____

_____

_____

_____

_____

_____

_____

_____

_____

_____

_____

_____

Titus' Report to Paul (2 Corinthians 7:5–7)

⁵ For indeed, when we came to Macedonia, our bodies had no rest, but we were troubled on every side. Outside were conflicts, inside were fears. ⁶ Nevertheless God, who comforts the downcast, comforted us by the coming of Titus, ⁷ and not only by his coming, but also by the consolation with which he was comforted in you, when he told us of your earnest desire, your mourning, your zeal for me, so that I rejoiced even more.

3. Paul now returns to his discussion of the "severe" or "sorrowful" letter that he mentioned writing (see 2:1–11). What was Paul's situation in Macedonia when he received the report back from Titus on how the Corinthians had received the letter (see verse 5)?

_____

_____

_____

_____

_____

_____

_____

_____

_____

_____

4. What effect did Titus say the letter had on the believers? What effect did this news have on the apostle Paul (see verses 6–7)?

_____

_____

_____

_____

_____

_____

_____

_____

_____

_____

_____

The Corinthians' Repentance (2 Corinthians 7:8–12)

⁸ For even if I made you sorry with my letter, I do not regret it; though I did regret it. For I perceive that the same epistle made you sorry, though only for a while. ⁹ Now I rejoice, not that you were made sorry, but that your sorrow led to repentance. For you were made sorry in a godly manner, that you might suffer loss from us in nothing. ¹⁰ For godly sorrow produces repentance leading to salvation, not to be regretted; but the sorrow of the world produces death. ¹¹ For observe this very thing, that you sorrowed in a godly manner: What diligence it produced in you, what clearing of yourselves, what indignation, what fear, what vehement desire, what zeal, what vindication! In all things you proved yourselves to be clear in this matter. ¹² Therefore, although I wrote to you, I did not do it for the sake of him who had done the wrong, nor for the sake of him who suffered wrong, but that our care for you in the sight of God might appear to you.

5. Paul's "severe letter" had caused a degree of distress on the believers. In spite of this, why did Paul say that he did not regret writing it (see verses 7–10)?

6. What did Paul say the believers' godly sorrow would produce in them (see verses 11–12)?

_____

_____

_____

_____

_____

_____

_____

_____

_____

_____

_____

_____

_____

_____

_____

The Joy of Titus (2 Corinthians 7:13–16)

¹³ Therefore we have been comforted in your comfort. And we rejoiced exceedingly more for the joy of Titus, because his spirit has been refreshed by you all. ¹⁴ For if in anything I have boasted to him about you, I am not ashamed. But as we spoke all things to you in truth, even so our boasting to Titus was found true. ¹⁵ And his affections are greater for you as he remembers the obedience of you all, how with fear and trembling you received him. ¹⁶ Therefore I rejoice that I have confidence in you in everything.

7. Paul has thus far described his own joy (and relief) at hearing the Corinthians had responded favorably to his "severe letter." But how did Titus feel after he spent time with the Corinthian believers (see verse 13)?

_____

_____

_____

_____

_____

_____

_____

8. Paul had "boasted" to Titus about the church in Corinth—and now they had proved that his high opinion of them was justified. What was it about the believers in Corinth that caused Titus to feel especially affectionate toward them (see verses 14–15)?

_____

_____

_____

_____

_____

_____

REVIEWING THE STORY

Paul reminded the believers in Corinth of the promises they had received from God and again appealed for them to open their hearts to him. He stated that he had done nothing to deserve their criticism and made it that he didn't want to condemn them but restore his fellowship with them. Paul then expressed his joy at receiving the good news from Titus that the believers had responded well to his "severe letter." He recognized that his letter had caused them distress but did not apologize for his words. After all, that sorrow had led to their repentance. He ended the chapter by recalling Titus's personal love and affection for the Corinthians.

9. What did Paul encourage the Corinthian believers to do (see 2 Corinthians 7:1)?

_____

_____

_____

_____

_____

10. What condition was Paul in when he came to Macedonia (see 2 Corinthians 7:5)?

_____

_____

_____

_____

_____

11. What is the difference between godly sorrow and the sorrow of the world (see 2 Corinthians 7:10)?

_____

_____

_____

_____

_____

12. What did Paul rejoice about concerning the Corinthian Christians (see 2 Corinthians 7:16)?

_____

_____

_____

_____

_____

_____

_____

APPLYING THE MESSAGE

13. When was the last time you felt genuine sorrow over something that you did?

_____

_____

_____

_____

_____

_____

_____

14. What are some of the positive effects that godly sorrow has produced in your life?

_____

_____

_____

_____

_____

_____

REFLECTING ON THE MEANING

Paul told the Corinthian believers, "For even if I made you sorry with my letter, I do not regret it" (2 Corinthians 7:8). After all he had nothing to regret, for he was speaking the truth about them in love. If we follow Paul's example and likewise speak God's truth in love, there is a good chance we will have to deal with offended reactions and hurt feelings—just as Paul did. When this occurs, we need to keep the following points in mind.

First, *we need to remember we are responsible for the message but not the response.* In one of Jesus' parables, he compared spreading the message of the gospel to a farmer sowing seeds (see Matthew 13:1–9, 18–23). The seed either flourished or failed depending on the ground (people's hearts) on which it fell. The farmer was not responsible for the outcome—just for sowing the seeds.

Second, *we need to remember that popularity is overrated.* Generally speaking, the more that we try to please other people in our lives, the less that we will seek to please God. Popularity can alter our perspectives and our priorities. Those who desire it will be tempted to compromise their principles to *attain* it, while those who have popularity will be tempted to compromise their principles in order to *maintain* it. For Christians, such compromises can damage our witness and cause us to miss out on God's plans for our lives. As Jesus put it, "For what profit is it to a man if he gains the whole world, and is himself destroyed or lost?" (Luke 9:25).

Third, *we need to remember that godly sorrow is good.* Sorrow is often the result of the Holy Spirit's work in our conscience—our realization that something is wrong. Sorrow is the motivation for us to change and compels us to admit our wrongdoing, ask for forgiveness, and restore our relationship with God. When this occurs in our hearts, what was once painful becomes something joyous.

This is the exact message that Paul wanted the believers in Corinth to understand.

JOURNALING YOUR RESPONSE

What is the hardest thing about speaking the truth in love?

HOW TO GIVE

2 Corinthians 8:1–24

GETTING STARTED

Why do you think the Bible places such a high priority on giving to others?

_____

_____

_____

_____

_____

_____

_____

_____

_____

_____

_____

_____

_____

_____

_____

_____

_____

_____

_____

_____

_____

_____

SETTING THE STAGE

One of the causes that was near and dear to Paul's heart was the collection for the poor in Jerusalem. The believers in that city were suffering as a result of a severe famine, crippling Roman and Jewish taxation, and general persecution and ostracization from society. Paul saw the opportunity for the wealthier Gentile churches to demonstrate true Christian love by "crossing the divide" and giving to their needy Jewish counterparts.

Paul had previously instructed the Corinthians to be diligent about making sure this collection was moving forward (see 1 Corinthians 16:1–2). Yet the efforts had apparently stalled as a result of the opponents of Paul who had been able to persuade many in the church to question the apostle's authority and motives. But now that reconciliation seems near, Paul takes the opportunity to remind the believers to keep up the collection . . . and in the process offers one of the most potent lessons on giving found in all of Scripture.

In Paul's appeal, he lifts up the giving spirit of the churches in Macedonia as the model to which other churches should aspire. He writes that in spite of "a great trial of affliction," these churches had given to the poor, "and their deep poverty abounded in the riches of their liberality" (8:2). The Macedonians gave not only *according* to their ability but also *beyond* their ability. In other words, these people had sacrificed greatly in order to give.

You cannot study any of Paul's letters without coming to the conclusion that such sacrificial giving was very much a part of the early church. It was not just a matter of tithing but a matter of purposeful, deliberate, consistent, cheerful, and thankful giving. The kind of giving that Paul describes means giving up something we want to do something God wants us to do.

EXPLORING THE TEXT

An Example of Giving (2 Corinthians 8:1–7)

---

¹ Moreover, brethren, we make known to you the grace of God bestowed on the churches of Macedonia: ² that in a great trial of affliction the

abundance of their joy and their deep poverty abounded in the riches of their liberality. ³ For I bear witness that according to their ability, yes, and beyond their ability, they were freely willing, ⁴ imploring us with much urgency that we would receive the gift and the fellowship of the ministering to the saints. ⁵ And not only as we had hoped, but they first gave themselves to the Lord, and then to us by the will of God. ⁶ So we urged Titus, that as he had begun, so he would also complete this grace in you as well. ⁷ But as you abound in every-thing—in faith, in speech, in knowledge, in all diligence, and in your love for us—see that you abound in this grace also.

1. Paul strategically begins this next section not with an appeal but with an example. What circumstances were the churches in Macedonia facing as Paul was collecting for the Christians in Jerusalem? How does Paul describe their spirit in giving (see verses 1–4)?

2. The believers in Macedonia went beyond Paul's expectations not only in their giving but in their willingness to give themselves to the cause. What is the lesson that Paul wants the believers in Corinth to take away from their example (see verses 5–7)?

_____

_____

_____

_____

_____

_____

_____

_____

_____

_____

_____

_____

_____

Christ Our Pattern (2 Corinthians 8:8–12)

⁸ I speak not by commandment, but I am testing the sincerity of your love by the diligence of others. ⁹ For you know the grace of our Lord Jesus Christ, that though He was rich, yet for your sakes He became poor, that you through His poverty might become rich.

¹⁰ And in this I give advice: It is to your advantage not only to be doing what you began and were desiring to do a year ago; ¹¹ but now you also must complete the doing of it; that as there was a readiness to desire it, so there also may be a completion out of what you have. ¹² For if there is first a willing mind, it is accepted according to what one has, and not according to what he does not have.

3. Paul is clear that he is not *instructing* the believers to give but asking them to willingly partner with him in the effort. Why would an instruction to give have defeated his purpose? What did he call on the believers to remember about Jesus (see verses 8–9)?

_____

_____

_____

_____

_____

_____

_____

4. How does Paul say the believers will benefit as a result of their giving (see verses 10–12)?

_____

_____

_____

_____

_____

_____

_____

Equality in the Church (2 Corinthians 8:13–15)

13 For I do not mean that others should be eased and you burdened; 14 but by an equality, that now at this time your abundance may supply their lack, that their abundance also may supply your lack—that there may be equality. 15 As it is written, "He who gathered much had nothing left over, and he who gathered little had no lack."

5. What potential misconception about giving did Paul want to clear up (see verses 13–14)?

_____

_____

_____

_____

_____

_____

_____

_____

6. The verse that Paul quotes from Exodus refers to the story of God giving manna to the Israelites in the wilderness. God distributed the resources equally and instructed no one to try to hoard the food. How do you think this supports Paul's claim that there should likewise be equality in sharing resources in the church (see verse 15)?

_____

_____

_____

_____

_____

_____

_____

_____

_____

Collection for the Judean Saints (2 Corinthians 8:16–24)

¹⁶ But thanks be to God who puts the same earnest care for you into the heart of Titus. ¹⁷ For he not only accepted the exhortation, but being more diligent, he went to you of his own accord. ¹⁸ And we have sent with him the brother whose praise is in the gospel

throughout all the churches, [19] and not only that, but who was also chosen by the churches to travel with us with this gift, which is administered by us to the glory of the Lord Himself and to show your ready mind, [20] avoiding this: that anyone should blame us in this lavish gift which is administered by us—[21] providing honorable things, not only in the sight of the Lord, but also in the sight of men.

[22] And we have sent with them our brother whom we have often proved diligent in many things, but now much more diligent, because of the great confidence which we have in you. [23] If anyone inquires about Titus, he is my partner and fellow worker concerning you. Or if our brethren are inquired about, they are messengers of the churches, the glory of Christ. [24] Therefore show to them, and before the churches, the proof of your love and of our boasting on your behalf.

7. Paul includes these words to show that he has appointed Titus and other delegates to serve as his representatives for the collection. Why was Titus the ideal candidate to collect the offering from the believers (see verses 16–17)?

8. Why did Paul appoint Titus (and the other unnamed delegates) to collect the money from the Corinthians instead of collecting it himself (see verse 20)?

_____

_____

_____

_____

_____

REVIEWING THE STORY

Paul offered the Corinthians examples and encouragement in giving. He began with the example of the churches in Macedonia, who, in spite of facing trials and poverty, were giving sacrificially to help the Christians in Jerusalem. Paul urged the Corinthians to take inspiration from their example and give generously. The apostle offered Jesus as a second example of giving. As deity, Christ was rich. But when He became human, He became poor—for our sake. Through His poverty, we can also become spiritually rich. Paul closed the chapter by urging the Corinthians to follow through on their previous willingness to give, to understand the cause to which they were giving, and to receive his delegates.

9. What was the Macedonian churches' order of priority in their giving (see 2 Corinthians 8:5)?

_____

_____

_____

_____

_____

10. What advice did Paul offer concerning the Corinthian Christians' previous willingness to give (see 2 Corinthians 8:10–11)?

_____

_____

_____

_____

_____

_____

_____

11. What potential for equality did Paul see in the Jerusalem church's spiritual abundance and the Corinthian church's material abundance (see 2 Corinthians 8:14)?

_____

_____

_____

_____

_____

_____

_____

12. What instructions did Paul give the Corinthians for when Titus and the unnamed brother in Christ arrived (see 2 Corinthians 8:24)?

_____

_____

_____

_____

_____

_____

_____

APPLYING THE MESSAGE

13. What obstacles keep believers in Christ from being more generous with their resources?

_____

_____

_____

_____

_____

_____

_____

_____

_____

_____

_____

_____

14. What is your attitude toward giving? What can you do to give more to God's work?

_____

_____

_____

_____

_____

_____

_____

_____

_____

_____

_____

_____

REFLECTING ON THE MEANING

In this section of the letter, Paul draws on the example of the churches in Macedonia to demonstrate what could be called "grace giving." This type of giving is sacrificial but encompasses several other important features.

First, *grace giving is spontaneous*. As the apostle Paul wrote, the believers in the Macedonian churches gave "not grudgingly or of necessity" (2 Corinthians 9:7). Rather, the Christians in those communities gave willingly and were excited about the prospects of doing so. They earnestly desired to be involved in the project.

Second, *grace giving is selfless*. Paul wrote that the belieers in the Macedonian churches "were freely willing, imploring us with much urgency that we would receive the gift and the fellowship of the ministering to the saints" (verses 3–4). Human nature usually finds its focus in its own needs, but grace giving always focuses on the needs of others. Grace giving always looks to how God is going to be able to use what we give to help others find Christ or grow in Him.

Third, grace giving is *systematic*. Paul wrote, "We urged Titus, that as he had begun, so he would also complete this grace in you as well" (8:6). The missionaries spent a whole year planning for the offering. They made sure it was organized and put together right, and when the time came for it to be collected, they made sure they had competent people to deliver it. Notice that this system began with a *commitment*. The believers could not wait until the time was "right" to give or until they felt they could afford to give. In the same way, grace giving will require us to be committed to the process . . . and to keep moving forward.

Finally, *grace giving is spiritual*. Giving is not a necessary evil or something we have to do to pay the bills. Rather it is just as much a part of our spiritual lives as Bible reading, prayer, and witnessing. We see this is true when we read that Paul encouraged the believers in Corinth to "abound in this grace also" (8:7). For Paul, stewardship was on the same level as any of the other spiritual disciplines that we find in the New Testament. It is a spiritual exercise.

JOURNALING YOUR RESPONSE

How can you better practice this kind of sacrificial giving this week?

SOWING AND REAPING

2 Corinthians 9:1–15

GETTING STARTED

What are some of the ways you invest your time and energy to help others?

_____

_____

_____

_____

_____

_____

_____

_____

_____

_____

_____

_____

_____

_____

SETTING THE STAGE

In Paul's letter to the Galatians, he wrote, "Whatever a man sows, that he will also reap" (6:7). Paul was quoting a principle from God's law—and it is a principle that we see in countless areas of life. In the agricultural world, whatever you sow into a field will determine what you harvest. In technology, whatever you input into a system will determine the output you will receive. In finance, whatever investment you make will determine the amount of your return. In athletics, if you want to perform well, you have to put in the work to practice well.

The law of sowing and reaping is the law of the universe. Every day, we all live it out, whether we know it or not—and whether we believe in it or not. Every day, the way we respond to this law determines the kind of person we are becoming. The principle is often presented as a warning—"Don't do something bad, because it will come back to bite you." In the Bible, however, the principle is typically presented in positive terms as a promise. At its heart, the law of sowing and reaping is a principle of investment.

Given this, it only makes sense that Paul would incorporate this principle into his discussion on giving and stewardship. As previously mentioned, Paul did not want to coerce or shame the believers in Corinth into contributing to the collection for the poor in Jerusalem. Rather, he wanted them to give sacrificially (like the Macedonian churches) and with a cheerful heart. They could give with joy if they comprehended the law of sowing and reaping.

As Paul states it, "He who sows sparingly will also reap sparingly, and he who sows bountifully will also reap bountifully" (2 Corinthians 9:6). If we want to receive the bountiful harvest that God has in store for us, then we need to not be stingy in the seeds we sow. We need to give sacrificially, trusting God with the outcome and knowing that He will take what we sow and multiply it exponentially for His purposes and His kingdom.

EXPLORING THE TEXT

Administering the Gift (2 Corinthians 9:1–5)

¹ Now concerning the ministering to the saints, it is superfluous for me to write to you; ² for I know your willingness, about which I boast of you to the Macedonians, that Achaia was ready a year ago; and your

zeal has stirred up the majority. ³ Yet I have sent the brethren, lest our boasting of you should be in vain in this respect, that, as I said, you may be ready; ⁴ lest if some Macedonians come with me and find you unprepared, we (not to mention you!) should be ashamed of this confident boasting. ⁵ Therefore I thought it necessary to exhort the brethren to go to you ahead of time, and prepare your generous gift beforehand, which you had previously promised, that it may be ready as a matter of generosity and not as a grudging obligation.

---

1. The believers in Corinth had initially expressed great enthusiasm in the collection for Jerusalem. However, as time had passed, that willingness had not translated into actual funds being collected. What does Paul say that he boasted about when he was in Macedonia? What was his present concern about the collection (see verses 1–4)?

_____

_____

_____

_____

_____

2. What did Paul decide to do to make sure the collection was actually taken (see verse 5)?

_____

_____

_____

_____

_____

_____

Sowing and Reaping (2 Corinthians 9:6–8)

> [6] But this I say: He who sows sparingly will also reap sparingly, and he who sows bountifully will also reap bountifully. [7] So let each one give as he purposes in his heart, not grudgingly or of necessity; for God loves a cheerful giver. [8] And God is able to make all grace abound toward you, that you, always having all sufficiency in all things, may have an abundance for every good work.

3. Paul will now emphasize some of the rewards that come from giving generously. What reason does he provide for encouraging the believers to give bountifully (see verse 6)?

_____

_____

_____

_____

_____

_____

4. Why do you think God "loves a cheerful giver"? What does Paul state that God does for believers who give abundantly from a cheerful heart (see verses 7–8)?

_____

_____

_____

_____

_____

_____

God Provides the Increase (2 Corinthians 9:9–11)

⁹ As it is written:

> "He has dispersed abroad,
> He has given to the poor;
> His righteousness endures forever."

¹⁰ Now may He who supplies seed to the sower, and bread for food, supply and multiply the seed you have sown and increase the fruits of your righteousness, ¹¹ while you are enriched in everything for all liberality, which causes thanksgiving through us to God.

5. What does Paul's quotation from Psalm 112:9 in this passage say about a cheerful giver's standing before God? What does Paul say will endure about such a person (see verse 9)?

_____

_____

_____

_____

_____

6. What does Paul say happens to those who are generous in their giving (see verses 10–11)?

_____

_____

_____

_____

_____

_____

The Cheerful Giver (2 Corinthians 9:12–15)

¹² For the administration of this service not only supplies the needs of the saints, but also is abounding through many thanksgivings to God, ¹³ while, through the proof of this ministry, they glorify God for the obedience of your confession to the gospel of Christ, and for your liberal sharing with them and all men, ¹⁴ and by their prayer for you, who long for you because of the exceeding grace of God in you. ¹⁵ Thanks be to God for His indescribable gift!

7. What are some of the more practical benefits that the believers in Corinth will experience if they choose to give cheerfully and generously (see verse 12)?

_____

_____

_____

_____

_____

_____

8. What did Paul say the gift would cause the recipients in Jerusalem to do (see verses 13–14)?

_____

_____

_____

_____

_____

_____

REVIEWING THE STORY

Paul reminded the believers in Corinth of their willingness to partner with him in taking up the collection for the poor in Jerusalem. However, he was concerned that his "boasting" about them to the Macedonians would be in vain if they did not deliver on their enthusiasm, so he was sending Titus (and other delegates) to make sure the plans for the collection were progressing. Paul reminded the believers that bountiful giving is rewarded bountifully and emphasized the importance of giving from a cheerful heart. He prayed for God's blessing on the generous Corinthians and listed many benefits they would receive for their acts of giving.

9. Why did Paul think it was necessary to send ahead his brothers in Christ to the Corinthian church (see 2 Corinthians 9:3–5)?

_____

_____

_____

_____

10. According to Paul, what does God love (see 2 Corinthians 9:7)?

_____

_____

_____

_____

11. How did Paul connect God's role in farming to His role in our giving (see 2 Corinthians 9:10)?

_____

_____

_____

_____

12. What four benefits of generous giving did Paul identify (see 2 Corinthians 9:12–14)?

APPLYING THE MESSAGE

13. What are some ways you can become a more cheerful giver?

---

14. What are some ways you have been blessed by giving to others?

REFLECTING ON THE MEANING

In this section of Paul's letter, we uncover four principles that we need to understand about sowing and reaping. The first is the *principle of investment*. As Paul wrote, "He who sows sparingly will also reap sparingly, and he who sows bountifully will also reap bountifully" (2 Corinthians 9:6). You do not reap if you merely *think* about sowing. You do not reap if you simply *pray* about sowing. You do not reap if you only *talk* about sowing.

Nor do you reap if you just *read a book* about somebody else sowing. You only reap if you sow!

The second is the *principle of identity*. In Paul's letter to the Galatians, he wrote, "For he who sows to his flesh will of the flesh reap corruption, but he who sows to the Spirit will of the Spirit reap everlasting life" (6:8). The type of harvest you will receive is determined by the kind of seed you sow. In the world of agriculture, if you sow barley, you get barley. If you sow wheat, expect wheat. If you sow a bad seed, you will get a bad crop. If you sow good seed, you will get a good crop. The nature of the seed dictates the nature of the harvest.

The third is the *principle of increase*. Paul wrote, "Now may He who supplies seed to the sower, and bread for food, supply and multiply the seed you have sown and increase the fruits of your righteousness" (2 Corinthians 9:10). When a farmer plants a seed, he naturally expects to receive something greater in return when the time comes for the harvest. If the seed just stayed the same, the whole process would be futile. In the same way, when you give generously, you can expect something greater in return. You can depend on God to turn your investment into something bigger and better than what you originally gave Him.

The fourth is the *principle of interval*. Paul wrote, "Let us not grow weary while doing good, for in due season we shall reap if we do not lose heart" (Galatians 6:9). Farmers know the harvest doesn't happen overnight—it takes time for a crop to mature. The same is true of the harvest God wants to reap in your life. At times, as you wait, you might get frustrated or impatient. You are sowing, but it doesn't appear the harvest is coming.

But it is in these times that the apostle Paul urges you to continue sowing and expecting God to reap the harvest. You continue to sow because God has promised that in due season you will reap. There is no *if, maybe*, or *possibly* in this promise—it is unconditional. And God will use these crucial times of waiting to help you grow and mature in your faith. This is why Paul could write, "Therefore, my beloved brethren, be steadfast, immovable, always abounding in the work of the Lord, knowing that your labor is not in vain in the Lord" (1 Corinthians 15:58).

JOURNALING YOUR RESPONSE

Which of these four principles is the hardest for you to understand or to embrace? Why?

THE SPIRITUAL WAR

2 Corinthians 10:1–18

GETTING STARTED

When was the last time you felt as though you were in a spiritual battle?

SETTING THE STAGE

All biblical scholars recognize there is an abrupt shift in Paul's tone as he moves into this next section of his letter. While there are different theories as to the cause of this shift, the most likely explanation is that 2 Corinthians 1–9 was written in one stage and, a short while later, Paul received some distressing news that caused him to pick up his pen and add 2 Corinthians 10–13. Once again, the issue at stake is the attempt within the church to discredit him.

Paul sees this opposition as a spiritual war. This war was being raged not only outside the walls of the church but also from within. Paul knew there were those in the Corinthian fellowship who were rebelling against his leadership and tearing down his reputation. His claim is that if a war is necessary to prove his accusers are wrong, he will not back away from it.

For many believers today, this confrontation is worrying. They do not believe a Christian leader—filled with the love of God—should be as confrontational as Paul is in this section of his letter. But Paul understands what is at stake. This is a war raging for the very hearts and minds of the believers in Corinth . . . and they are in immense danger. As he states, "For though we walk in the flesh, we do not war according to the flesh. For the weapons of our warfare are not carnal but mighty in God for pulling down strongholds, casting down arguments and every high thing that exalts itself against the knowledge of God" (2 Corinthians 10:3–5).

This battle for the mind is too critical for him to tiptoe around. These strongholds of the mind must be fought and overthrown. This is what we find the apostle doing as he begins his final section of the letter.

EXPLORING THE TEXT

Bold and Meek (2 Corinthians 10:1–3)

> ¹ Now I, Paul, myself am pleading with you by the meekness and gentleness of Christ—who in presence am lowly among you,

but being absent am bold toward you. ² But I beg you that when I am present I may not be bold with that confidence by which I intend to be bold against some, who think of us as if we walked according to the flesh. ³ For though we walk in the flesh, we do not war according to the flesh.

1. Paul had been accused of being bold at a distance (in writing his letters) but meek when he was in the believers' presence. What does he say about the meekness and gentleness that he displays? What does he want to avoid on his next visit (see verses 1–2)?

_____

_____

_____

_____

2. Paul wanted to avoid a confrontation with those in the church but was ready to defend his authority if needed. What does he mean when he says that he does not "war according to the flesh"? To what type of war is he referring (see verse 3)?

_____

_____

_____

_____

Paul's Spiritual Weapons (2 Corinthians 10:4–6)

⁴ For the weapons of our warfare are not carnal but mighty in God for pulling down strongholds, ⁵ casting down arguments and every high thing that exalts itself against the knowledge of God, bringing

every thought into captivity to the obedience of Christ, [6] and being ready to punish all disobedience when your obedience is fulfilled.

---

3. Paul states that he does not rely on earthly weapons in this war for the believers' minds but on the divine weapons of God. What can these weapons do (see verses 4–5)?

_____

_____

_____

_____

_____

4. Why was it critical for the believers to bring "every thought into captivity to the obedience of Christ"? What should be our goal when it comes to our thoughts (see verses 5–6)?

_____

_____

_____

_____

The Reality of Paul's Authority (2 Corinthians 10:7–11)

[7] Do you look at things according to the outward appearance? If anyone is convinced in himself that he is Christ's, let him again consider this in himself, that just as he is Christ's, even so we are Christ's. [8] For even if I should boast somewhat more about our authority, which the Lord gave us for edification and not for your destruction, I shall not be ashamed—[9] lest I seem to terrify you by letters. [10] "For his letters," they say, "are weighty and powerful, but his bodily presence is weak, and his speech contemptible." [11] Let such a person consider

this, that what we are in word by letters when we are absent, such we will also be in deed when we are present.

---

5. Paul's opponents continued to try to undermine his authority as an apostle of Christ. What does Paul suggest they do before they judge him (see verse 7)?

_____

_____

_____

_____

_____

6. What were Paul's opponents saying about his manner when he was with the Corinthians? How does Paul respond to this accusation (see verses 10–11)?

_____

_____

_____

_____

_____

The Limits of Paul's Authority (2 Corinthians 10:12–18)

[12] For we dare not class ourselves or compare ourselves with those who commend themselves. But they, measuring themselves by themselves, and comparing themselves among themselves, are not wise. [13] We, however, will not boast beyond measure, but within the limits of the sphere which God appointed us—a sphere which especially includes you. [14] For we are not overextending ourselves (as though our authority did not extend to you), for it was to you that we came

with the gospel of Christ; [15] not boasting of things beyond measure, that is, in other men's labors, but having hope, that as your faith is increased, we shall be greatly enlarged by you in our sphere, [16] to preach the gospel in the regions beyond you, and not to boast in another man's sphere of accomplishment.

[17] But "he who glories, let him glory in the LORD." [18] For not he who commends himself is approved, but whom the Lord commends.

---

7. Paul now speaks out directly against "those who commend themselves"—his opponents who had infiltrated the church in Corinth. What does Paul say these individuals boast about? What is Paul only willing to boast about (see verses 12–13)?

---

8. Paul asserts that his opponents were priding themselves on the work done by others. How were Paul and his coworkers different? What was their goal (see verses 14–16)?

REVIEWING THE STORY

Paul received further news of his opponents' actions in Corinth and picked up his pen to address their latest accusations against him. He stated that while he seemed meek in person, he was ready to be bold with those who had made these claims. Paul saw this struggle as a spiritual battle for the hearts and minds of the believers and was ready to employ the spiritual weapons of warfare in the fight. Paul then confronted the troublemakers about their misplaced priorities and shared his perspective of his authority as an apostle. He warned the believers to be careful what they wished for, as they might just get the bold version of himself the next time he visited. He ended by examining the right and wrong ways to measure ministry.

9. What was the nature of the apostle Paul's plea to the Corinthians (see 2 Corinthians 10:1–2)?

10. What are four things that spiritual weapons can accomplish (see 2 Corinthians 10:4–6)?

11. For what purpose did the Lord give Paul his spiritual authority (see 2 Corinthians 10:8)?

12. To whom did the apostle Paul say that he did not want to compare himself (see 2 Corinthians 10:12)?

APPLYING THE MESSAGE

13. What thoughts are hardest for you to bring "into captivity to the obedience of Christ"?

14. What's the best strategy for bringing those thoughts into captivity?

REFLECTING ON THE MEANING

In this passage, Paul uses a military analogy to talk about his capacity to defend himself against the attacks of his opponents. There are four key points we can take away from his words. First, *we have a dangerous enemy*. Peter warned, "Be sober, be vigilant; because your adversary the devil walks about like a roaring lion, seeking whom he may devour" (1 Peter 5:8). Any area of our lives can become a battlefield when our enemy sees an opportunity. As Peter states, this is why we must be vigilant. As dangerous as our enemy is, he is no match for our Ally.

Second, *our battles should not be taken lightly*. Many heroes of the faith suffered severe setbacks when they let down their guard or underestimated their opponent. Peter inadvertently did Satan's work when he challenged Jesus' prediction of His crucifixion (see Matthew 16:21–23). Later, a few unnamed disciples thought they could drive a demon out of a boy but discovered that they could not (see 17:14–21). Luke writes that Satan entered Judas Iscariot and caused him to betray Jesus to His enemies (see 22:3).

Third, *we need to arm ourselves for the conflict*. In his letter to the Ephesians, Paul encouraged believers to "put on the whole armor of God," including the breastplate of righteousness, the shield of faith, and the sword of the Spirit (see 6:11–18). Part of our preparation involves identifying our vulnerable spots. For instance, if we know we are vulnerable to gossip, we need to remove ourselves from places where rumors flow freely.

Fourth, *resistance is not futile*. James says, "Resist the devil and he will flee from you" (4:7). We resist the devil by asking God for His help and by studying His Word. When Satan tempted Jesus in the wilderness, the Lord countered his attacks by quoting Scripture. Jesus' example reveals that the more of the Bible we commit to memory, the better equipped we will be to counter Satan's attacks. We also resist the enemy by not giving him a foothold. We turn our back on temptation the moment it occurs or address our doubts the moment we experience them. We do this because we know the longer we allow negative emotions to hang around, the more entrenched they become in our lives.

JOURNALING YOUR RESPONSE

What is your most effective strategy when it comes to resisting the enemy's attacks against you?

GOD IS OUR STRENGTH

2 Corinthians 11:1–33

GETTING STARTED

What are some of the qualities that you look for in a leader?

_____

_____

_____

_____

_____

_____

_____

_____

_____

_____

_____

_____

_____

_____

_____

_____

_____

_____

_____

_____

_____

SETTING THE STAGE

In 1967, psychiatrist Dr. Thomas Holmes created a test we know as the Holmes-Rahe Stress Inventory. The scale provided a simple measurement as to how stress affects a person. It also predicted the way in which that stress could cause illnesses in an individual's life.

In creating the test, Dr. Holmes considered various changes and situations and gave each a numerical value, assigning points for the amount of stress it caused. Some of these included the death of a spouse (100 points), being fired from a job (47 points), having a baby (39 points), vacations (13 points), and Christmas (12 points). According to Dr. Holmes, when a person reached 200 points, that person was in deep trouble.

Today we can only wonder at how many points the apostle Paul would have accumulated! In this next section of his letter, he describes how he was beaten (five times), shipwrecked (three times), in constant peril on journeys, robbed, persecuted (frequently), and weary and hungry (often). He also describes the stress that came from being concerned about the state of the churches that he had helped to found.

Paul was able to weather these hardships because he didn't look to his own power to survive them. He looked to the power of the Holy Spirit living within him. Paul had grown inwardly as he was assailed outwardly. In the same way, we can be assured no matter what troubles we face, we can trust God to be with us in the midst of them. However, like Paul, we need to take steps now—before the trials come—to strengthen our relationship with God so we can understand what it means to rely on His strength.

EXPLORING THE TEXT

Concern for the Believers' Faithfulness (2 Corinthians 11:1–4)

¹ Oh, that you would bear with me in a little folly—and indeed you do bear with me. ² For I am jealous for you with godly jealousy. For I have betrothed you to one husband, that I may present you as a

chaste virgin to Christ. ³ But I fear, lest somehow, as the serpent deceived Eve by his craftiness, so your minds may be corrupted from the simplicity that is in Christ. ⁴ For if he who comes preaches another Jesus whom we have not preached, or if you receive a different spirit which you have not received, or a different gospel which you have not accepted—you may well put up with it!

1. Paul has pointed out the folly in his opponents' self-praise, but he realizes a bit of self-praise on his own part is needed if he wants to defend himself against the charges laid against him. What does he go on to say about the way he feels about the believers (see verses 1–2)?

2. Why was Paul concerned about the believers' attitudes toward the false teachers who were promoting "another Jesus" than the one he had taught (see verses 3–4)?

A Burden to None (2 Corinthians 11:5–11)

⁵ For I consider that I am not at all inferior to the most eminent apostles. ⁶ Even though I am untrained in speech, yet I am not in knowledge. But we have been thoroughly manifested among you in all things.

⁷ Did I commit sin in humbling myself that you might be exalted, because I preached the gospel of God to you free of charge? ⁸ I robbed other churches, taking wages from them to minister to you. ⁹ And when I was present with you, and in need, I was a burden to no one, for what I lacked the brethren who came from Macedonia supplied. And in everything I kept myself from being burdensome to you, and so I will keep myself. ¹⁰ As the truth of Christ is in me, no one shall stop me from this boasting in the regions of Achaia. ¹¹ Why? Because I do not love you? God knows!

3. Paul, still engaging in a bit of "self-praise," bluntly states that he does not consider himself inferior to even the most eminent apostles. What reason did he give to support this claim? Why did he choose to be humble in the believers' midst (see verses 5–7)?

_____

_____

_____

_____

_____

_____

_____

_____

_____

_____

4. Ironically, the apostle Paul had evidently received criticism for *not* accepting money for the churches in which he was ministering, as was the practice of other itinerant preachers. How does he defend himself against this charge (see verses 8–11)?

_____

_____

_____

_____

_____

_____

_____

Reluctant Boasting (2 Corinthians 11:12–21)

¹² But what I do, I will also continue to do, that I may cut off the opportunity from those who desire an opportunity to be regarded just as we are in the things of which they boast. ¹³ For such are false apostles, deceitful workers, transforming themselves into apostles of Christ. ¹⁴ And no wonder! For Satan himself transforms himself into an angel of light. ¹⁵ Therefore it is no great thing if his ministers also transform themselves into ministers of righteousness, whose end will be according to their works.

¹⁶ I say again, let no one think me a fool. If otherwise, at least receive me as a fool, that I also may boast a little. ¹⁷ What I speak, I speak not according to the Lord, but as it were, foolishly, in this confidence of boasting. ¹⁸ Seeing that many boast according to the flesh, I also will boast. ¹⁹ For you put up with fools gladly, since you yourselves are wise! ²⁰ For you put up with it if one brings you into bondage, if one devours you, if one takes from you, if one exalts himself, if one strikes you on the face. ²¹ To our shame I say that we were too weak for that! But in whatever anyone is bold—I speak foolishly—I am bold also.

5. How does Paul describe those who were ridiculing him, questioning his authority, and preaching another message of the gospel other than the one he was proclaiming? In what way did Paul see this as a spiritual battle (see verses 12–15)?

_____

_____

_____

_____

_____

_____

_____

6. Paul states that he has defended himself by boasting in the same manner as his opponents. What criticism does Paul level against the believers for listening to those who boast? What will happen to those who follow such false teachers (see verses 16–21)?

_____

_____

_____

_____

_____

_____

_____

_____

Suffering for Christ (2 Corinthians 11:22–33)

22 Are they Hebrews? So am I. Are they Israelites? So am I. Are they the seed of Abraham? So am I. 23 Are they ministers of Christ?— I speak as a fool—I am more: in labors more abundant, in stripes

above measure, in prisons more frequently, in deaths often. ^{24} From the Jews five times I received forty stripes minus one. ^{25} Three times I was beaten with rods; once I was stoned; three times I was shipwrecked; a night and a day I have been in the deep; ^{26} in journeys often, in perils of waters, in perils of robbers, in perils of my own countrymen, in perils of the Gentiles, in perils in the city, in perils in the wilderness, in perils in the sea, in perils among false brethren; ^{27} in weariness and toil, in sleeplessness often, in hunger and thirst, in fastings often, in cold and nakedness—^{28} besides the other things, what comes upon me daily: my deep concern for all the churches. ^{29} Who is weak, and I am not weak? Who is made to stumble, and I do not burn with indignation?

^{30} If I must boast, I will boast in the things which concern my infirmity. ^{31} The God and Father of our Lord Jesus Christ, who is blessed forever, knows that I am not lying. ^{32} In Damascus the governor, under Aretas the king, was guarding the city of the Damascenes with a garrison, desiring to arrest me; ^{33} but I was let down in a basket through a window in the wall, and escaped from his hands.

---

7. Paul now begins to compare himself to the false teachers who had infiltrated Corinth. What does Paul say about his credentials as it relates to his Jewish heritage (see verses 22–23)?

_____

_____

_____

_____

_____

_____

_____

_____

_____

_____

8. What do you think is the purpose that Paul had in mind for recounting all of the hardships that he had faced? What comparisons is he again making here as it relates to his ministry and the ministries of those who were attacking him (see verses 24–33)?

_____

_____

_____

_____

_____

_____

_____

_____

_____

_____

_____

_____

_____

_____

_____

_____

REVIEWING THE STORY

Paul asked the believers to permit him a little "folly" as he engaged in some self-praise in order to defend himself. He spoke of his fear about the Corinthians' faithfulness and bluntly stated that he was not inferior to any other apostle. He explained his reasons for humbling himself in their midst and not accepting financial support from them. He then confronted the Corinthians about their preference for false apostles and encouraged them to recognize the sincerity and truth of his message. Paul ended this section as he began it—laying out his impressive credentials as a Jew and as an apostle, even though he felt foolish about doing so.

9. What motivated Paul to present his credentials as an apostle to the Corinthian believers (see 2 Corinthians 11:2)?

_____

_____

_____

_____

_____

_____

10. How did Paul summarize the strength and weakness of his ministry skill set (see 2 Corinthians 11:6)?

_____

_____

_____

_____

_____

_____

11. Why was Paul unconcerned about looking foolish in the eyes of the Corinthians (see 2 Corinthians 11:19)?

_____

_____

_____

_____

_____

_____

12. What did Paul prefer to boast about (see 2 Corinthians 11:30)?

APPLYING THE MESSAGE

13. What situations or circumstances are causing stress in your life right now? How do Paul's words in this section encourage you?

14. How can you keep your reputation intact so that you can be a powerful witness for Christ?

REFLECTING ON THE MEANING

When Paul spoke of the "inward" person (see 2 Corinthians 4:16), he was speaking of the *soul* or *spirit*—the center of our personality where the Holy Spirit and Christ reside. The key to standing strong in the midst of stress is to strengthen the inward person. This way, we can face whatever life brings our way because the strength with which God fills us meets the test. The problem is that we live in an *outward* world and the inward tends to get lost in the shuffle.

There are several reasons for this. The first reason is that *we do not have a proper appreciation for eternity*. The Bible says the inward part of us lives on through eternity. The soul we have now is the same soul we will have throughout eternity. So, as we build the inward person, we are building that part of us that is eternal.

The second reason is that *we do not have God's perspective on life*. The world tells us that the most important thing we possess is our body. We must keep it beautiful, strong, and young . . . because it *is* everything. If we're not careful, we may allow the world to squeeze us into its mold. In contrast, God's emphasis is on the inward person. He looks at the heart.

The third reason is that *we do not value the inward person*. We live in an accomplishment-oriented society, and spending time alone with God to build the inward person does not show up on a task list or accomplishment chart. So, instead we spend our time doing outward things—putting on a good show and creating a great shell. Inside, however, we may be feeling empty, because nobody cares to ask us how he are doing inwardly.

Our responsibility is to push past these obstacles and to strengthen our trust in God in every area of life. We do this by studying His Word, spending time in prayer, and simply remaining silent before Him so that He can speak into our hearts. We fight against the enemies of the soul—the attitudes, the obstacles, and the distractions that keep us from focusing inward—knowing that the more we invest in our relationship with God right now, the more we will be able to rest and trust in Him when future struggles come.

JOURNALING YOUR RESPONSE

What steps will you take to ensure that you are looking to God and His strength to give you what you need in every future situation?

GOD'S GRACE IN OUR WEAKNESS

2 Corinthians 12:1–21

GETTING STARTED

How might a physical weakness actually serve to make a person stronger on the inside?

SETTING THE STAGE

The apostle Paul loved to employ paradoxes—seeming contradictions in terms—to relate certain spiritual truths to his readers. Earlier in this letter, he talked about finding comfort through suffering (see 1:3–7), glory through shame (see 3:7–18), and life through death (see 4:7–15). These apparently contradictory statements lay at the core of Paul's concept of Christianity—phrases that tug at our intellect and make us ask, "What could this mean?"

The topic that Paul chooses to discuss in this next section of his letter—finding strength in weakness—could also be considered a paradox of the Christian faith. The apostle begins with an extraordinary personal experience. By divine appointment, God lifted him up to see the glories of heaven. The experience was so incredible that Paul did not have adequate words to explain it. He also did not want to boast in relating the experience—something he had accused his opponents of doing—so he wrote in the third person: "I know a man . . . [who] was caught up to the third heaven" (2 Corinthians 12:2). But he was speaking about himself.

Paul wasn't willing to tell everything that had happened to him during this event. Maybe he was not even capable of relating all that had happened. But what Paul *did* know is that on this occasion, because of divine appointment, he had been lifted up to see the glories of heaven that no person had ever seen before. Furthermore, something happened as a result of that experience that Paul could not possibly have predicted. He experienced a profound *weakness* in his life—and then found extraordinary *strength* as a result.

EXPLORING THE TEXT

A Vision of Paradise (2 Corinthians 12:1–6)

[1] It is doubtless not profitable for me to boast. I will come to visions and revelations of the Lord: [2] I know a man in Christ who fourteen

years ago—whether in the body I do not know, or whether out of the body I do not know, God knows—such a one was caught up to the third heaven. ³ And I know such a man—whether in the body or out of the body I do not know, God knows—⁴ how he was caught up into Paradise and heard inexpressible words, which it is not lawful for a man to utter. ⁵ Of such a one I will boast; yet of myself I will not boast, except in my infirmities. ⁶ For though I might desire to boast, I will not be a fool; for I will speak the truth. But I refrain, lest anyone should think of me above what he sees me to be or hears from me.

1. Paul reiterates it is not his desire to boast about his spiritual exploits. However, he feels the need to highlight a specific revelation that he received from the Lord some fourteen years before. How does Paul describe this vision (see verses 1–4)?

_____

_____

_____

_____

_____

2. Of what was Paul willing to boast? Why was he careful to only boast about what Jesus had done in his life rather than about any of his own accomplishments (see verses 5–6)?

_____

_____

_____

_____

_____

_____

The Thorn in the Flesh (2 Corinthians 12:7–10)

---

[7] And lest I should be exalted above measure by the abundance of the revelations, a thorn in the flesh was given to me, a messenger of Satan to buffet me, lest I be exalted above measure. [8] Concerning this thing I pleaded with the Lord three times that it might depart from me. [9] And He said to me, "My grace is sufficient for you, for My strength is made perfect in weakness." Therefore most gladly I will rather boast in my infirmities, that the power of Christ may rest upon me. [10] Therefore I take pleasure in infirmities, in reproaches, in needs, in persecutions, in distresses, for Christ's sake. For when I am weak, then I am strong.

---

3. Paul was aware that such a special revelation could lead him to believing that he was "more spiritual" than others. What happened to prevent this attitude from forming (see verse 7)?

_____

_____

_____

_____

4. Biblical scholars debate as the nature of Paul's "thorn in the flesh," but this could refer to anxiety, opposition to his ministry, or a physical ailment. Regardless, why did God refuse to take away this thorn? What did He want Paul to understand (see verses 8–10)?

_____

_____

_____

_____

Signs of an Apostle (2 Corinthians 12:11–13)

11 I have become a fool in boasting; you have compelled me. For I ought to have been commended by you; for in nothing was I behind the most eminent apostles, though I am nothing. 12 Truly the signs of an apostle were accomplished among you with all perseverance, in signs and wonders and mighty deeds. 13 For what is it in which you were inferior to other churches, except that I myself was not burdensome to you? Forgive me this wrong!

5. Paul finds it distasteful that he had to boast about himself at all in order to fight back against his opponents. What does he say should have happened instead (see verse 11)?

_____

_____

_____

_____

_____

_____

6. What does Paul ask the believers to remember about his ministry in Corinth? What was the one difference between him and the other "eminent apostles" (see verses 12–13)?

_____

_____

_____

_____

_____

Love for the Church (2 Corinthians 12:14–21)

¹⁴ Now for the third time I am ready to come to you. And I will not be burdensome to you; for I do not seek yours, but you. For the children ought not to lay up for the parents, but the parents for the children. ¹⁵ And I will very gladly spend and be spent for your souls; though the more abundantly I love you, the less I am loved.

¹⁶ But be that as it may, I did not burden you. Nevertheless, being crafty, I caught you by cunning! ¹⁷ Did I take advantage of you by any of those whom I sent to you? ¹⁸ I urged Titus, and sent our brother with him. Did Titus take advantage of you? Did we not walk in the same spirit? Did we not walk in the same steps?

¹⁹ Again, do you think that we excuse ourselves to you? We speak before God in Christ. But we do all things, beloved, for your edification. ²⁰ For I fear lest, when I come, I shall not find you such as I wish, and that I shall be found by you such as you do not wish; lest there be contentions, jealousies, outbursts of wrath, selfish ambitions, backbitings, whisperings, conceits, tumults; ²¹ lest, when I come again, my God will humble me among you, and I shall mourn for many who have sinned before and have not repented of the uncleanness, fornication, and lewdness which they have practiced.

---

7. Paul states that he is preparing for his third visit to the believers in Corinth. Why does he state that he will continue to not accept money from them (see verses 14–18)?

_____

_____

_____

_____

_____

8. Paul notes that he only finds it necessary to defend his conduct before God—and not before any person on earth. Given this, why did he choose to write this personal defense in his letter? What is he hoping his words will accomplish (see verses 19–21)?

_____

_____

_____

_____

_____

_____

REVIEWING THE STORY

Paul acknowledged it was not profitable for him to boast. However, he felt compelled to share a vision from God that had been given to him. Paul was taken to heaven, where he saw and heard things that he could not put into words. Although he could have become conceited at the prospects of receiving such a personal revelation, the Lord allowed him to be afflicted with an unidentified "thorn in the flesh" to maintain his humility. Paul prayed three times to have the thorn removed, but God said no—He would provide for Paul through his thorn. Paul wrapped up his "boasting" and announced his intention to make another trip to Corinth.

9. How did Paul refer to himself as he described his vision (see 2 Corinthians 12:2)?

_____

_____

_____

_____

_____

10. Why did Paul say that he would rather boast in his infirmities (see 2 Corinthians 12:9)?

_____

_____

_____

_____

11. What did Paul say the Corinthian believers should have done when the "eminent apostles" started questioning his credentials (see 2 Corinthians 12:11)?

_____

_____

_____

12. What hurtful realization did Paul share with the Corinthian believers (see 2 Corinthians 12:15)?

_____

_____

_____

_____

APPLYING THE MESSAGE

13. What are some "thorns in the flesh" that you have experienced?

_____

_____

_____

_____

14. What is the best strategy for dealing with your thorn in the flesh?

_____

_____

_____

_____

_____

REFLECTING ON THE MEANING

When I am weak, then I am strong. This is a simple principle that can change your entire outlook on life. It is during those times when you are feeling weak or confused that God is working behind the scenes in your life. He is preparing you to be used for His purposes.

Paul understood the importance of living by this principle. When he traveled to Corinth for the first time, he had just left the city of Athens. His experience there had been unpleasant, to say the least, as the highly educated Athenians had rejected his message. So, on his way to Corinth—a city with an equally daunting reputation for intellectualism—the apostle decided he would not come "with excellence of speech or of wisdom . . . [but] in weakness, in fear, and in much trembling" (1 Corinthians 2:1, 3).

As a result, some of those in Corinth criticized Paul for not matching the oratory and sophistication of their great leaders and speakers. Paul embraced their criticism and said, "You're right. I'm not impressive. All I am is a servant of Almighty God. I'm so weak that if God hadn't done something through me, *nothing* would have happened." Paul understood that God only uses people when they are dependent on Him. So he chose to look to God for his strength so that the Lord could work in his life.

Paul's example reveals that while no one is too weak for God to use, there are many people who are too *strong* for God to use. This is why you must approach God with a humble heart. When you encounter times of struggle and weakness, your best strategy is to say, "Lord, what are You going to do in my life through this time? Whatever it is, I am okay with

125

it. Show Yourself strong in my weakness. Use me during this time." Then step back, trust God to do the work, and see where He leads you next.

Journaling Your Response

Why is it often so hard to embrace our particular weaknesses?

EXAMINE YOURSELVES

2 Corinthians 13:1–14

GETTING STARTED

When was the last time you reconnected with someone in person, not knowing whether the encounter would be pleasant or unpleasant?

_____

_____

_____

_____

_____

_____

_____

_____

_____

_____

_____

_____

_____

_____

_____

_____

_____

_____

SETTING THE STAGE

Paul's primary aim in writing the letter of 2 Corinthians was to defend his authority and credentials as an apostle. Yet in this pursuit he was not being egocentric or insecure. Rather, he wanted the Corinthians to be able to recognize the "real deal" when they saw it. This is why he stressed that God had called him to be an evangelist. Why he provided details about his scholarship in Jewish law and personal recognition of God's grace. Why he spoke of the beatings, imprisonments, and persecutions that he had endured. Why he called out the false apostles in their midst.

Paul wanted the believers to see what the true ministry of an apostle involved. It meant making yourself available to answer the church members' questions. Challenging and encouraging the members even when you could not be present. Providing your own financial means as a tentmaker so the congregation would not be burdened. Embracing the idea of being a Christian role model and opening your life to scrutiny. Maintaining the ability to have a humble and contrite spirit in the midst of it all.

The Corinthians should have rejoiced to have Paul as a mentor and guide. But the problem was that Paul did not look, speak, or act like the other apostles who had come to the city. In comparison to their slick appearance, Paul's ministry seemed *amateurish*. Paul saw this as a problem not because it tarnished his reputation but because he knew this attitude would continue to lead them into error. So, in this final section of his letter, he puts forth one more challenge to get the believers on the right track: compelling them to examine their faith.

EXPLORING THE TEXT

Coming with Authority (2 Corinthians 13:1–4)

[1] This will be the third time I am coming to you. "By the mouth of two or three witnesses every word shall be established." [2] I have told you before, and foretell as if I were present the second time, and now

being absent I write to those who have sinned before, and to all the rest, that if I come again I will not spare—³ since you seek a proof of Christ speaking in me, who is not weak toward you, but mighty in you. ⁴ For though He was crucified in weakness, yet He lives by the power of God. For we also are weak in Him, but we shall live with Him by the power of God toward you.

---

1. Paul was clearly feeling a pang of anxiety and personal foreboding as he considered the prospects of making a third visit to Corinth. What did he warn would happen if he found the church was still wallowing in decisiveness and immorality (see verses 1–3)?

_____

_____

_____

_____

_____

_____

_____

2. How did Paul compare his actions with those of Christ? What was Paul implying about how power can be manifested in apparent weakness (see verse 4)?

_____

_____

_____

_____

_____

_____

_____

The Need for Self-Examination (2 Corinthians 13:5–6)

> [5] Examine yourselves as to whether you are in the faith. Test your-selves. Do you not know yourselves, that Jesus Christ is in you?—unless indeed you are disqualified. [6] But I trust that you will know that we are not disqualified.

3. The Corinthians had been looking for "proof" that Jesus Christ was operating through Paul. How does the apostle say they should have been able to recognize this truth (see verse 5)?

_____

_____

_____

_____

_____

_____

4. What do you think it means to "test yourself" so you can determine "whether you are in the faith"? What does it mean to be "disqualified" in this respect (see verses 5–6)?

_____

_____

_____

_____

_____

_____

_____

Gentleness Is Preferred (2 Corinthians 13:7–10)

7 Now I pray to God that you do no evil, not that we should appear approved, but that you should do what is honorable, though we may seem disqualified. 8 For we can do nothing against the truth, but for the truth. 9 For we are glad when we are weak and you are strong. And this also we pray, that you may be made complete. 10 Therefore I write these things being absent, lest being present I should use sharpness, according to the authority which the Lord has given me for edification and not for destruction.

5. What did Paul want the believers in Corinth to do even if his words in this letter did not persuade them that he could be trusted (see verse 7)?

_____

_____

_____

_____

_____

_____

6. How did Paul summarize his mission to the church? Why did he say that he was writing out these instructions now—before he arrived (see verses 8–10)?

_____

_____

_____

_____

_____

Greetings and Benediction (2 Corinthians 13:11–14)

¹¹ Finally, brethren, farewell. Become complete. Be of good comfort, be of one mind, live in peace; and the God of love and peace will be with you.

¹² Greet one another with a holy kiss.

¹³ All the saints greet you.

¹⁴ The grace of the Lord Jesus Christ, and the love of God, and the communion of the Holy Spirit be with you all. Amen.

7. Paul is now ready to move to his final closing and blessing on the believers. What final appeal does he make to them (see verses 11–12)?

_____

_____

_____

_____

_____

_____

8. How did Paul remind the Corinthians that they weren't alone in their faith (see verses 13–14)?

_____

_____

_____

_____

_____

_____

_____

_____

REVIEWING THE STORY

Paul concludes his lengthy second letter to the Corinthians by instructing them to examine themselves before he arrived. He made it plain that he would come with all the power of Christ's judgment if they did not address their sin—so they needed to consider what they truly believed and whether the light of Jesus was within them. He acknowledged that if people judged a genuine Christian life by worldly standards, that individual would seem to be *disqualified*. Yet Paul pointed out that if his weakness could make the Corinthians strong, he would be glad of it. Paul ended the letter with his familiar exhortations and greetings.

9. What comparison did the apostle Paul make between himself and Christ (see 2 Corinthians 13:4)?

_____

_____

_____

_____

_____

_____

_____

10. What was the first examination that Paul wanted the Corinthians to perform on themselves (see 2 Corinthians 13:5)?

_____

_____

_____

_____

_____

_____

_____

11. What was Paul's real concern for the believers in Corinth (see 2 Corinthians 13:9)?

_____

_____

_____

_____

_____

12. What final four instructions did Paul give the Corinthian believers (see 2 Corinthians 13:11)?

_____

_____

_____

_____

_____

APPLYING THE MESSAGE

13. What questions should people ask to determine whether they are truly followers of Christ?

_____

_____

_____

_____

_____

14. How can you pray for others in the way that Paul prayed for the believers in Corinth?

_____

_____

_____

_____

_____

REFLECTING ON THE MEANING

Imagine that you are going to write a letter like the ones the apostle Paul wrote. The purpose of your letter is to encourage other Christians—perhaps new believers—and help them grow in their faith. You want to equip them for their walk with Christ. You want to confront them about issues that may become stumbling blocks for them. You want to warn them about Satan's tactics and strategies. You want to help them see what they are doing right—and how God will bless their efforts. You want to establish yourself as someone who can and will help them. How would you go about doing this?

Your first step would be to *identify your recipients and present your credentials*. You would structure your arguments based on what you believe would appeal the most to your audience and provide your credentials to them. Paul was often questioned as to why people should listen to him. He always answered with absolute humility but never downplayed the authority and calling that God had given him to proclaim the gospel. In the same way, you can never downplay the gifts God has given you or the hard-earned wisdom you have acquired.

Your next step would be to *consider the content*. What spiritual topics are closest to your heart? What wisdom would you impart? What lessons from your life would you share? What would you confront your readers about? What warnings would you send?

Finally, you would *consider your closing*. What final thoughts would you want your readers to take away? What greetings would you send? What compliments or blessings would you offer to them?

You may never be comfortable enough with your literary skills to write a letter like the apostle Paul did for the churches in which he ministered. But it can be a helpful exercise to consider the possibility. If you have been a Christian for a while, you have experience, perspective, and wisdom that is valuable to other people. You also have the encouragement of the Holy Spirit to share what you have with others—perhaps as a mentor, a Bible study partner, or a Sunday school teacher.

Journaling Your Response

How can you share your God-given experiences, perspective, and wisdom with others?

LEADER'S GUIDE

Thank you for choosing to lead your group through this study from Dr. David Jeremiah on *The Letter of 2 Corinthians*. Being a group leader has its own rewards, and it is our prayer that your walk with the Lord will deepen through this experience. During the twelve lessons in this study, you and your group will read selected passages from 2 Corinthians, explore key themes in the letter based on teachings from Dr. Jeremiah, and review questions that will encourage group discussion. There are multiple components in this section that can help you structure your lessons and discussion time, so please be sure to read and consider each one.

BEFORE YOU BEGIN

Before your first meeting, make sure you and your group are well-versed with the content of the lesson. Group members should have their own copy of *The Letter of 2 Corinthians* study guide prior to the first meeting so they can follow along and record their answers, thoughts, and insights. After the first week, you may wish to assign the study guide lesson as homework prior to the group meeting and then use the meeting time to discuss the content in the lesson.

To ensure everyone has a chance to participate in the discussion, the ideal size for a group is around eight to ten people. If there are more than ten people, break up the bigger group into smaller subgroups. Make sure the members are committed to participating each week, as this will help create stability and help you better prepare the structure of the meeting.

At the beginning of each week's study, start with the opening Getting Started question to introduce the topic you will be discussing. The members should answer briefly, as the goal is just for them to have an idea of the subject in their minds as you go over the lesson. This will allow the members to become engaged and ready to interact with the rest of the group.

After reviewing the lesson, try to initiate a free-flowing discussion. Invite group members to bring questions and insights they may have discovered to the next meeting, especially if they were unsure of the meaning of some parts of the lesson. Be prepared to discuss how biblical truth applies to the world we live in today.

WEEKLY PREPARATION

As the group leader, here are a few things that you can do to prepare for each meeting:

- *Be thoroughly familiar with the material in the lesson.* Make sure that you understand the content of each lesson so you know how to structure the group time and are prepared to lead the group discussion.

- *Decide, ahead of time, which questions you want to discuss.* Depending on how much time you have each week, you may not be able to reflect on every question. Select specific questions that you feel will evoke the best discussion.

- *Take prayer requests.* At the end of your discussion, take prayer requests from your group members and then pray for one another.

STRUCTURING THE DISCUSSION TIME

There are several ways to structure the duration of the study. You can choose to cover each lesson individually, for a total of twelve weeks of group meetings, or you can combine two lessons together per week, for a total of six weeks of group meetings. The following charts illustrates these options:

TWELVE-WEEK FORMAT

Week	Lessons Covered	Reading
1	A Question of Sincerity	2 Corinthians 1:1–24
2	Identified with Christ	2 Corinthians 2:1–3:18
3	Treasure in Earthen Vessels	2 Corinthians 4:1–18
4	The Gospel of Reconciliation	2 Corinthians 5:1–21
5	Unequally Yoked	2 Corinthians 6:1–18
6	Speaking the Truth in Love	2 Corinthians 7:1–16
7	How to Give	2 Corinthians 8:1–24
8	Sowing and Reaping	2 Corinthians 9:1–15
9	The Spiritual War	2 Corinthians 10:1–18
10	God Is Our Strength	2 Corinthians 11:1–33
11	God's Grace in Our Weakness	2 Corinthians 12:1–21
12	Examine Yourselves	2 Corinthians 13:1–14

SIX-WEEK FORMAT

Week	Lessons Covered	Reading
1	A Question of Sincerity / Identified with Christ	2 Corinthians 1:1–3:18
2	Treasure in Earthen Vessels / The Gospel of Reconciliation	2 Corinthians 4:1–5:21
3	Unequally Yoked / Speaking the Truth in Love	2 Corinthians 6:1–7:16
4	How to Give / Sowing and Reaping	2 Corinthians 8:1–9:15
5	The Spiritual War / God Is Our Strength	2 Corinthians 10:1–11:33
6	God's Grace in Our Weakness / Examine Yourselves	2 Corinthians 12:1–13:14

In regard to organizing your time when planning your group Bible study, the following two schedules, for sixty minutes and ninety minutes, can give you a structure for the lesson:

Section	60 Minutes	90 Minutes
Welcome: Members arrive and get settled	5 minutes	10 minutes
Getting Started Question: Prepares the group for interacting with one another	10 minutes	10 minutes
Message: Review the lesson	15 minutes	25 minutes
Discussion: Discuss questions in the lesson	25 minutes	35 minutes
Review and Prayer: Review the key points of the lesson and have a closing time of prayer	5 minutes	10 minutes

As the group leader, it is up to you to keep track of the time and keep things moving according to your schedule. If your group is having a good discussion, don't feel the need to stop and move on to the next question. Remember, the purpose is to pull together ideas and share unique insights on the lesson. Encourage everyone to participate, but don't be concerned if certain group members are more quiet. They may just be internally reflecting on the questions and need time to process their ideas before they can share them.

GROUP DYNAMICS

Leading a group study can be a rewarding experience for you and your group members—but that doesn't mean there won't be challenges. Certain members may feel uncomfortable discussing topics that they consider very personal and might be afraid of being called on. Some members might have disagreements on specific issues. To help prevent these scenarios, consider the following ground rules:

- If someone has a question that may seem off topic, suggest that it be discussed at another time, or ask the group if they are okay with addressing that topic.

- If someone asks a question you don't know the answer to, confess that you don't know and move on. If you feel comfortable, invite other group members to give their opinions or share their comments based on personal experience.
- If you feel like a couple of people are talking much more than others, direct questions to people who may not have shared yet. You could even ask the more dominating members to help draw out the quiet ones.
- When there is a disagreement, encourage the group members to process the matter in love. Invite members from opposing sides to evaluate their opinions and consider the ideas of the other members. Lead the group through Scripture that addresses the topic, and look for common ground.

When issues arise, encourage your group to think of Scripture: "Love one another" (John 13:34), "If it is possible, as much as it depends on you, live peaceably with all men" (Romans 12:18), and, "Be swift to hear, slow to speak, slow to wrath" (James 1:19).

ABOUT
Dr. David Jeremiah and Turning Point

Dr. David Jeremiah is the founder of Turning Point, a ministry committed to providing Christians with sound Bible teaching relevant to today's changing times through radio and television broadcasts, audio series, books, and live events. Dr. Jeremiah's teaching on topics such as family, prayer, worship, angels, and biblical prophecy forms the foundation of Turning Point.

David and his wife, Donna, reside in El Cajon, California, where he serves as the senior pastor of Shadow Mountain Community Church. David and Donna have four children and twelve grandchildren.

In 1982, Dr. Jeremiah brought the same solid teaching to San Diego television that he shares weekly with his congregation. Shortly thereafter, Turning Point expanded its ministry to radio. Dr. Jeremiah's inspiring messages can now be heard worldwide on radio, television, and the internet.

Because Dr. Jeremiah desires to know his listening audience, he travels nationwide holding ministry rallies and spiritual enrichment conferences that touch the hearts and lives of many people. According to Dr. Jeremiah, "At some point in time, everyone reaches a turning point; and for every person, that moment is unique, an experience to hold onto forever. There's so much changing in today's world that sometimes it's difficult to choose the right path. Turning Point offers people an understanding of God's Word and seeks to make a difference in their lives."

Dr. Jeremiah has authored numerous books, including *Escape the Coming Night* (Revelation), *The Handwriting on the Wall* (Daniel), *Overcoming Loneliness*, *Prayer—The Great Adventure*, *God in You* (Holy Spirit), *When*

Your World Falls Apart, Slaying the Giants in Your Life, My Heart's Desire, Hope for Today, Captured by Grace, Signs of Life, What in the World Is Going On?, The Coming Economic Armageddon, I Never Thought I'd See the Day!, God Loves You: He Always Has—He Always Will, Agents of the Apocalypse, Agents of Babylon, Revealing the Mysteries of Heaven, People Are Asking . . . Is This the End?, A Life Beyond Amazing, Overcomer, and *The Book of Signs.*

STAY CONNECTED
to Dr. David Jeremiah

Take advantage of two great ways to let Dr. David Jeremiah give you spiritual direction every day!

Turning Points Magazine and Devotional

Receive Dr. David Jeremiah's magazine, *Turning Points*, each month and discover:

- Thematic study focus
- 48 pages of life-changing reading
- Relevant articles
- Special features
- Daily devotional readings
- Bible study resource offers
- Live event schedule
- Radio & television information

Request *Turning Points* magazine today!

(800) 947-1993
www.DavidJeremiah.org/Magazine

Daily Turning Point E-Devotional

Start your day off right! Find words of inspiration and spiritual motivation waiting for you on your computer every morning! Receive a daily e-devotion communication from David Jeremiah that will strengthen your walk with God and encourage you to live the authentic Christian life.

Request your free e-devotional today!

(800) 947-1993
www.DavidJeremiah.org/Devo

New Bible Study Series
from Dr. David Jeremiah

The Jeremiah Bible Study Series captures Dr. David Jeremiah's
forty-plus years of commitment to teaching the whole Word of God.
Each volume contains twelve lessons for individuals and groups to
explore what the Bible says, what it meant to the people at the time it
was written, and what it means to us today. Out of his lifelong ministry
of *delivering the unchanging Word of God to an ever-changing world*,
Dr. Jeremiah has written this Bible-strong study series focused not on
causes, current events, or politics, but on the solid truth of Scripture.

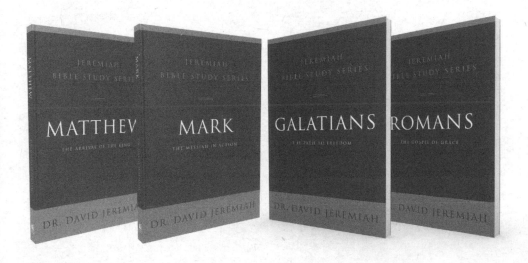

9780310091493	Matthew	9780310091554	John	9780310091646	1 Corinthians
9780310091516	Mark	9780310091608	Acts	9780310097488	2 Corinthians
9780310091530	Luke	9780310091622	Romans	9780310091660	Galatians

Available now at your favorite bookstore.
More volumes coming soon.

THOMAS NELSON
Since 1798